CGP's Mental Maths is as cool as your shades!

Summer is here! Whip out your sunglasses, apply some sun cream and get ready for your Mental Maths skills to sparkle in the summer sun...

This sizzling CGP book covers a wide range of skills from the Year 5 curriculum — there's a page of Mental Maths practice for every day of the summer term.

It's perfect for use in class or at home, with plenty of examples and splashes of colourful fun throughout to keep pupils entertained. Shine on!

What CGP is all about

Our sole aim here at CGP is to produce the highest quality books — carefully written, immaculately presented and dangerously close to being funny.

Then we work our socks off to get them out to you — at the cheapest possible prices.

Contents

☑ Use the tick boxes to help keep a record of which tests have been attempted.

Week 1
- ☑ Day 1 1
- ☑ Day 2 2
- ☑ Day 3 3
- ☑ Day 4 4
- ☑ Day 5 5

Week 2
- ☑ Day 1 6
- ☑ Day 2 7
- ☑ Day 3 8
- ☑ Day 4 9
- ☑ Day 5 10

Week 3
- ☑ Day 1 11
- ☑ Day 2 12
- ☑ Day 3 13
- ☑ Day 4 14
- ☑ Day 5 15

Week 4
- ☑ Day 1 16
- ☑ Day 2 17
- ☑ Day 3 18
- ☑ Day 4 19
- ☑ Day 5 20

Week 5
- ☑ Day 1 21
- ☑ Day 2 22
- ☑ Day 3 23
- ☑ Day 4 24
- ☑ Day 5 25

Week 6
- ☑ Day 1 26
- ☑ Day 2 27
- ☑ Day 3 28
- ☑ Day 4 29
- ☑ Day 5 30

Week 7
- ☑ Day 1 31
- ☑ Day 2 32
- ☑ Day 3 33
- ☑ Day 4 34
- ☑ Day 5 35

Week 8
- ☑ Day 1 36
- ☑ Day 2 37
- ☑ Day 3 38
- ☑ Day 4 39
- ☑ Day 5 40

Week 9
- [x] Day 1 41
- [x] Day 2 42
- [x] Day 3 43
- [x] Day 4 44
- [x] Day 5 45

Week 10
- [x] Day 1 46
- [x] Day 2 47
- [x] Day 3 48
- [x] Day 4 49
- [x] Day 5 50

Week 11
- [x] Day 1 51
- [x] Day 2 52
- [x] Day 3 53
- [x] Day 4 54
- [x] Day 5 55

Week 12
- [x] Day 1 56
- [x] Day 2 57
- [x] Day 3 58
- [x] Day 4 59
- [x] Day 5 60

Answers 61

Published by CGP

ISBN: 978 1 78908 774 1

Editors: Ellen Burton, Katherine Faudemer, Sarah Pattison, Claire Plowman, Tamara Sinivassen.

With thanks to Tina Ramsden and Glenn Rogers for the proofreading.

With thanks to Emily Smith for the copyright research.

Clipart from Corel®

Printed by Elanders Ltd, Newcastle upon Tyne.
Based on the classic CGP style created by Richard Parsons.

Text, design, layout and original illustrations © Coordination Group Publications Ltd. (CGP) 2022
All rights reserved.

Photocopying this book is not permitted, even if you have a CLA licence.
Extra copies are available from CGP with next day delivery • 0800 1712 712 • www.cgpbooks.co.uk

How to Use this Book

- This book contains 60 daily practice tests.
- We've split them into 12 sections — that's roughly one for each week of the Year 5 summer term.
- Each week is made up of 5 tests, so there's one for every school day of the term (Monday – Friday).
- Each test should take about 10 minutes to complete.
- Pupils should aim to do their working in their heads, without writing anything down.
- The tests contain a mix of Mental Maths topics from Year 5. New Year 5 topics are gradually introduced as you go through the book.
- The tests increase in difficulty as you progress through the term.
- The last three weeks recap Mental Maths topics from throughout Year 5.
- Each test looks something like this:

The Week and the Day of the test are shown at the top of the page.

The instruction the pupil needs to follow is in the box at the top of the page.

There's an example at the top of the page. The correct answer is shown in red. Talk the pupil through the instruction and the example so they know what to do.

There's a score box at the bottom of the test. Use this to keep track of how well the pupil has done.

There are between 4 and 14 questions for the pupil to answer.

Week 1 — Day 1

Fill in the box with the equivalent fraction or decimal. Give the fractions as tenths or hundredths so that they are in their simplest form.

$\frac{9}{10}$ = 0.9

1) $\frac{3}{10}$ = ☐

2) ☐ = 0.7

3) $\frac{8}{10}$ = ☐

4) ☐ = 0.1

5) $\frac{23}{100}$ = ☐

6) ☐ = 0.87

7) $\frac{51}{100}$ = ☐

8) ☐ = 0.73

9) $\frac{29}{100}$ = ☐

10) ☐ = 0.13

11) $\frac{2}{100}$ = ☐

12) ☐ = 0.01

Today I scored ☐ out of 12.

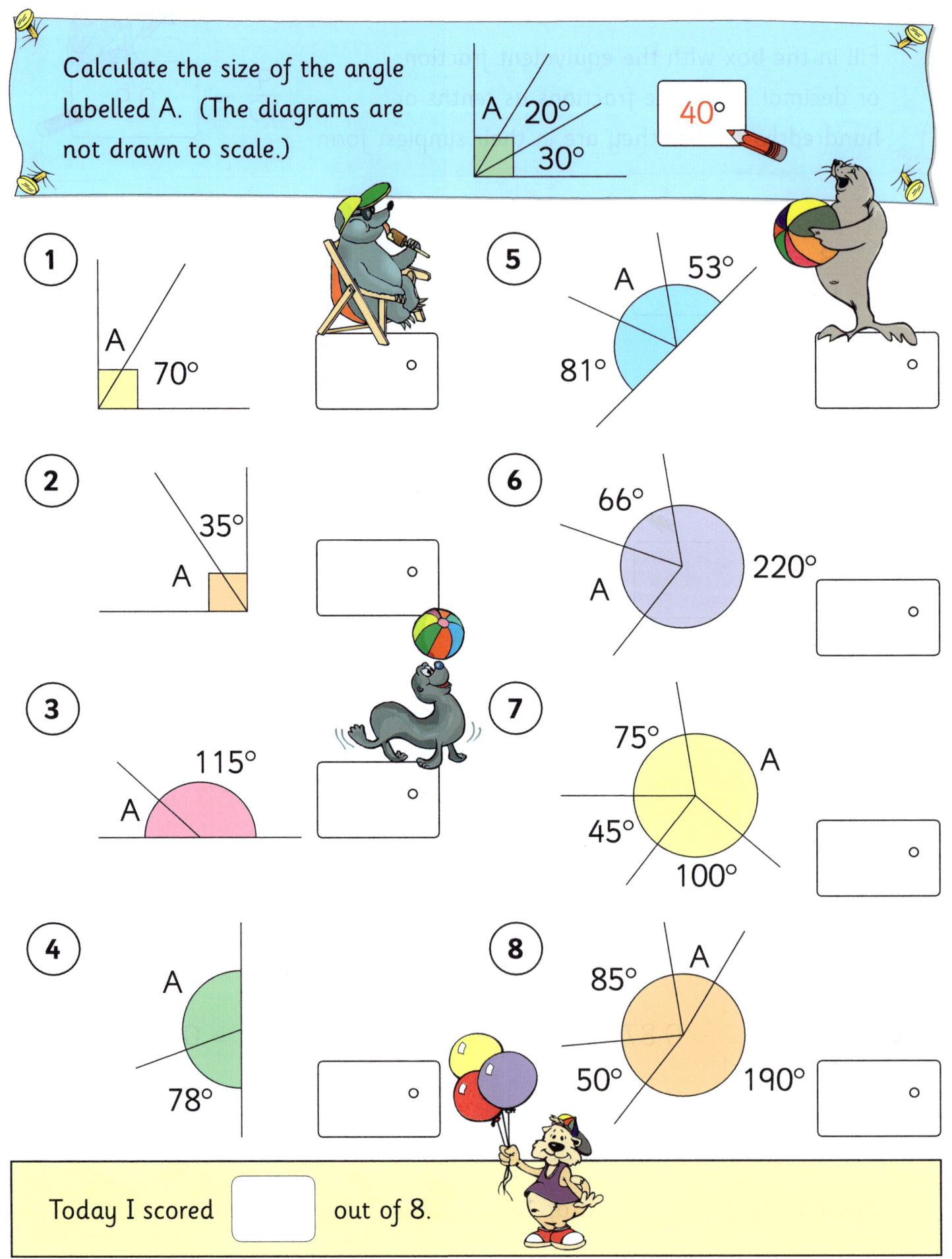

Week 1 — Day 3

Calculate the length of the tunnel.

Vole digs 2 km every hour. How long is his tunnel after 5 hours?

10 km

1) Mouse digs 4 km every 6 hours. How long is his tunnel after 12 hours?

____ km

2) Mole digs 3 km every 2 hours. How long is her tunnel after 10 hours?

____ km

3) Shrew digs 6 km every 5 hours. How long is his tunnel after 20 hours?

____ km

4) Rabbit digs 3 km every 8 hours. How long is her tunnel after 24 hours?

____ km

5) Badger digs 0.5 km every 20 minutes. How long is her tunnel after 1 hour?

____ km

6) Fox digs 200 m every 15 minutes. How long is his tunnel after 75 minutes?

____ km

7) Chipmunk digs 60 m every 30 minutes. How long is her tunnel after 5 hours?

____ km

8) Rat digs 900 m every hour. How long is his tunnel after 20 minutes?

____ km

Today I scored ____ out of 8.

Week 1 — Day 4

Toby is going shopping. How much will the fruit cost him?

£3.30 per 1 kg

500 g will cost Toby £1.65

1. £3.00 per 10 kg — 30 kg will cost Toby £
2. £0.30 per 200 g — 400 g will cost Toby £
3. £0.70 per 1 kg — 5 kg will cost Toby £
4. £0.40 per 90 g — 270 g will cost Toby £
5. £0.30 per 60 g — 360 g will cost Toby £
6. £0.40 per 150 g — 750 g will cost Toby £
7. £1.90 per 1 kg — 500 g will cost Toby £
8. £8.00 per 1 kg — 750 g will cost Toby £

Today I scored ☐ out of 8.

Week 1 — Day 5

Work out the pupil's score in their Maths test.

There were 100 marks in total.
Mia got 7 out of every 10 marks.
Mia got **70** out of 100.

1) There were 100 marks in total. Mat got 3 out of every 5 marks.
Mat got ☐ out of 100.

2) There were 150 marks in total. Meg got 2 out of every 3 marks.
Meg got ☐ out of 150.

3) There were 180 marks in total. Mae got 5 out of every 6 marks.
Mae got ☐ out of 180.

4) There were 84 marks in total. Mal got 3 out of every 7 marks.
Mal got ☐ out of 84.

5) There were 96 marks in total. Min got 6 out of every 8 marks.
Min got ☐ out of 96.

6) There were 121 marks in total. Mol got 9 out of every 11 marks.
Mol got ☐ out of 121.

7) There were 70 marks in total. Mel got 9 out of every 14 marks.
Mel got ☐ out of 70.

8) There were 175 marks in total. Mu got 21 out of every 25 marks.
Mu got ☐ out of 175.

9) There were 220 marks in total. Mi got 16 out of every 20 marks.
Mi got ☐ out of 220.

10) There were 110 marks in total. Mo got 15 out of every 22 marks.
Mo got ☐ out of 110.

Today I scored ☐ out of 10.

Week 2 — Day 1

Complete the calculation.   27 000 − 1500 = 25 500

1) 35 000 − 20 000 =

2) 12 000 + 32 000 =

3) 100 000 − 25 000 =

4) 13 000 + 2400 =

5) 75 100 − 20 100 =

6) 71 100 + 8200 =

7) 84 500 − 2100 =

8) 14 210 + 30 100 =

9) 16 100 − 1010 =

10) 54 124 + 4900 =

11) 14 000 − 3750 =

12) 155 203 + 4728 =

Today I scored ☐ out of 12.

Week 2 — Day 2

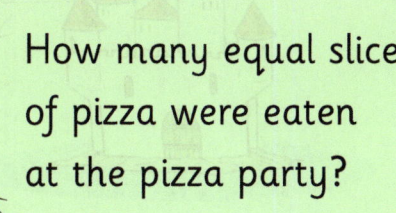
How many equal slices of pizza were eaten at the pizza party?

Each pizza was cut into 4 slices. 2 pizzas were eaten.

8 slices

1. Each pizza was cut into 6 slices. $1\frac{1}{2}$ pizzas were eaten. ☐ slices

2. Each pizza was cut into 20 slices. $\frac{3}{4}$ of a pizza was eaten. ☐ slices

3. Each pizza was cut into 18 slices. $\frac{1}{6}$ of a pizza was eaten. ☐ slices

4. Each pizza was cut into 12 slices. $\frac{2}{3}$ of a pizza was eaten. ☐ slices

5. Each pizza was cut into 8 slices. $2\frac{1}{2}$ pizzas were eaten. ☐ slices

6. Each pizza was cut into 5 slices. $1\frac{1}{5}$ pizzas were eaten. ☐ slices

7. Each pizza was cut into 7 slices. $5\frac{2}{7}$ pizzas were eaten. ☐ slices

8. Each pizza was cut into 10 slices. $1\frac{2}{5}$ pizzas were eaten. ☐ slices

9. Each pizza was cut into 25 slices. $2\frac{4}{5}$ pizzas were eaten. ☐ slices

10. Each pizza was cut into 9 slices. $2\frac{2}{3}$ pizzas were eaten. ☐ slices

11. Each pizza was cut into 24 slices. $1\frac{5}{6}$ pizzas were eaten. ☐ slices

12. Each pizza was cut into 15 slices. $2\frac{3}{5}$ pizzas were eaten. ☐ slices

Today I scored ☐ out of 12.

Week 2 — Day 3

The year is shown in Roman numerals. Write it in numbers. MCMXC → 1990

1) MMII
2) MDC
3) MCCCX
4) MCXX
5) MCCV
6) MMXIV
7) MIX
8) MMXXI
9) MCMLX
10) MDL
11) MCDLXXI
12) MCMLXXIX

Today I scored ___ out of 12.

Week 2 — Day 4

Fill in the number of hours. Write your answer as a mixed number when possible.

Dougal practises the cello for 30 minutes a day. How much time does he spend practising in 7 days? $3\frac{1}{2}$ hours

1. Nicola practises the guitar for 15 minutes a day. How much time does she spend practising in 6 days? ☐ hours

2. Saif practises the flute for 45 minutes a day. How much time does he spend practising in 2 days? ☐ hours

3. Mindy practises the trombone for 20 minutes a day. How much time does she spend practising in 6 days? ☐ hours

4. Geoff practises the drums for 1 hour 30 minutes a day. How much time does he spend practising in 3 days? ☐ hours

5. Bonnie practises the oboe for 1 hour 15 minutes a day. How much time does she spend practising in 7 days? ☐ hours

6. Helena practises the piano for 10 minutes a day. How much time does she spend practising in 8 days? ☐ hours

7. Devon practises the banjo for 1 hour 20 minutes a day. How much time does he spend practising in 6 days? ☐ hours

8. Iwan practises the harp for 40 minutes a day. How much time does he spend practising in 4 days? ☐ hours

Today I scored ☐ out of 8.

Week 2 — Day 5

Calculate the rectangle's perimeter. The shapes are not drawn to scale.

Side A is 3 cm. Side B is twice as long as side A.

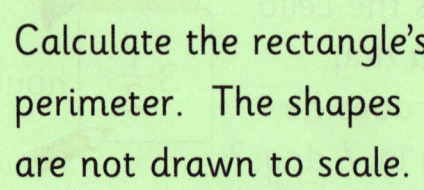
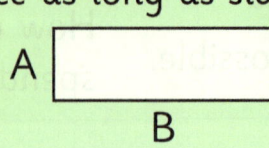

18 cm

1) Side B is 8 cm. Side A is half as long as side B.

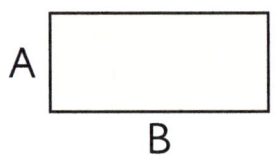 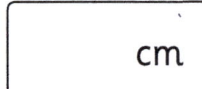 cm

5) Side A is 10 cm. Side B is three times as long as side A.

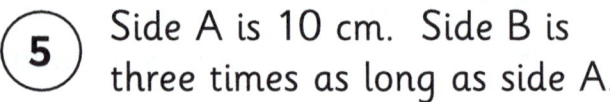 cm

2) Side A is 2.5 cm. Side B is the same length as side A.

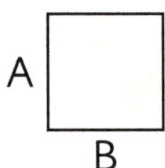 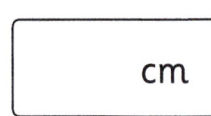 cm

6) Side B is 16 cm. Side A is one quarter of the length of side B.

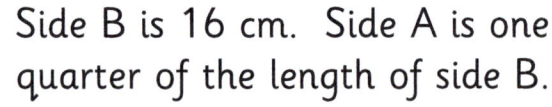 cm

3) Side B is 6 cm. Side A is one third of the length of side B.

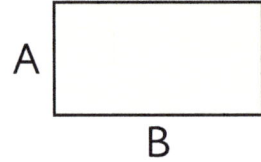 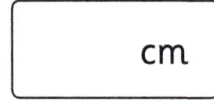 cm

7) Side B is 100 cm. Side A is two fifths of the length of side B.

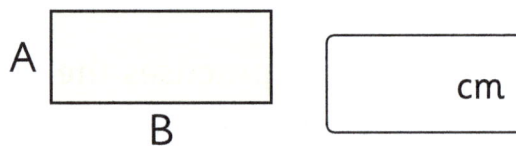 cm

4) Side A is 1.5 cm. Side B is twice as long as side A.

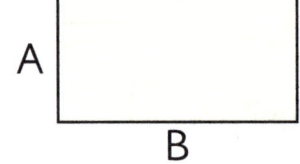  cm

8) Side A is 0.2 cm. Side B is four times as long as side A.

 cm

Today I scored ☐ out of 8.

Week 3 — Day 1

Fill in the missing numbers to complete the sentence about the properties of the shape.

An equilateral triangle has **3** equal sides and **3** equal angles.

1) A parallelogram has ☐ pair(s) of equal sides and ☐ pair(s) of parallel sides.

2) An isosceles triangle has ☐ equal sides and ☐ equal angles.

3) A regular octagon has ☐ equal sides and ☐ equal angles.

4) A scalene triangle has ☐ equal sides and ☐ equal angles.

5) A rectangle has ☐ pair(s) of parallel sides and ☐ right angles.

6) A rhombus has ☐ equal sides and ☐ pair(s) of parallel sides.

7) A kite has ☐ pair(s) of equal sides and ☐ pair(s) of parallel sides.

8) A trapezium has ☐ pair(s) of parallel sides and no more than ☐ pair(s) of equal sides.

Today I scored ☐ out of 8.

Week 3 — Day 2

The table shows the number of customers a barber shop had each month. Circle the two busiest months. Then calculate the total number of customers in those months.

Month	(April)	(May)	June
Customers	415	777	312

1192

1.
Month	March	April	May	June
Customers	2491	5105	3203	1005

2.
Month	March	April	May	June
Customers	910	1004	1040	1933

3.
Month	March	April	May	June
Customers	4312	3145	3451	3512

4.
Month	March	April	May	June
Customers	1316	1613	1336	1163

5.
Month	March	April	May	June
Customers	725	563	275	367

6.
Month	March	April	May	June
Customers	4231	2297	2329	2257

7.
Month	March	April	May	June
Customers	3915	3195	3390	3510

8.
Month	March	April	May	June
Customers	2255	2525	2552	2225

9.
Month	March	April	May	June
Customers	5433	5444	5344	5443

Today I scored ☐ out of 9.

Week 3 — Day 3

Fill in the missing number(s) to complete the sentence.

The prime factors of 20 are 2, 2 and ☐5☐.

1. The prime factors of 6 are 3 and ☐.

2. The prime factors of 15 are 3 and ☐.

3. The prime factors of 8 are 2, 2 and ☐.

4. The prime factors of 12 are 2, 2 and ☐.

5. The prime factors of 18 are 2, 3 and ☐.

6. The prime factors of 34 are 2 and ☐.

7. The prime factors of 28 are 7, ☐ and ☐.

8. The prime factors of 36 are 2, 3, ☐ and ☐.

9. The prime factors of 45 are 5, ☐ and ☐.

10. The prime factors of 54 are 2, 3, ☐ and ☐.

11. The prime factors of 48 are 2, 2, 2, ☐ and ☐.

12. The prime factors of 39 are ☐ and ☐.

Today I scored ☐ out of 12.

Week 3 — Day 4

1 m is approximately 3 ft.
5 miles is approximately 8 km.
Convert the distance travelled.

Sid the snail travelled 6 m. → 18 ft

1. Daisy the duck travelled 25 m. ☐ ft
2. Wendy the worm travelled 15 m. ☐ ft
3. Cai the caterpillar travelled 7.5 m. ☐ ft
4. Harold the hare travelled 1200 ft. ☐ m
5. Tia the tortoise travelled 180 ft. ☐ m
6. Noah the newt travelled 360 ft. ☐ m
7. Ruby the reindeer travelled 25 miles. ☐ km
8. Taj the tiger travelled 240 km. ☐ miles
9. Chipo the cheetah travelled 200 miles. ☐ km
10. Alf the alligator travelled 640 km. ☐ miles
11. Wilma the whale travelled 1500 miles. ☐ km
12. Zoe the zebra travelled 9600 km. ☐ miles

Today I scored ☐ out of 12.

Week 3 — Day 5

You are given three numbers.
Write each number in the table.
Use each number once only
and fill all rows in the table.

| 2 | 7 | 8 |

Prime number	7
Prime factor of 32	2
Composite number	8

1) | 5 | 6 | 13 |

Prime number	
Prime factor of 15	
Composite number	

2) | 10 | 7 | 2 |

Prime number	
Prime factor of 49	
Composite number	

3) | 3 | 4 | 11 |

Prime number	
Prime factor of 22	
Composite number	

4) | 17 | 15 | 3 |

Prime number	
Prime factor of 45	
Composite number	

5) | 5 | 9 | 3 |

Prime number	
Prime factor of 81	
Composite number	

6) | 12 | 5 | 19 |

Prime number	
Prime factor of 60	
Composite number	

7) | 14 | 3 | 11 |

Prime number	
Prime factor of 96	
Composite number	

8) | 21 | 23 | 19 |

Prime number	
Prime factor of 38	
Composite number	

Today I scored ☐ out of 8.

Week 4 — Day 1

Is the number in the star a square number, a cube number or neither?

 Square number ✓ Cube number ☐ Neither ☐

1.  ☐ Square number ☐ Cube number ☐ Neither

2.  ☐ Square number ☐ Cube number ☐ Neither

3.  ☐ Square number ☐ Cube number ☐ Neither

4.  ☐ Square number ☐ Cube number ☐ Neither

5.  ☐ Square number ☐ Cube number ☐ Neither

6.  ☐ Square number ☐ Cube number ☐ Neither

7.  ☐ Square number ☐ Cube number ☐ Neither

8.  ☐ Square number ☐ Cube number ☐ Neither

9.  ☐ Square number ☐ Cube number ☐ Neither

10. ☐ Square number ☐ Cube number ☐ Neither

Today I scored ☐ out of 10.

Year 5 Mental Maths — Summer Term   © CGP — Not to be photocopied

Week 4 — Day 2

Use the 24-hour clock to write the time the lesson finishes.

Freya's French lesson starts at 2:10 pm and lasts 1 hour 15 minutes.

15:25

1) Tom's technology lesson starts at 1:30 pm and lasts 45 minutes.

2) Haifa's history lesson starts at 8:35 am and lasts 30 minutes.

3) Gina's geography lesson starts at 12:25 pm and lasts 1 hour 5 minutes.

4) Luke's literacy lesson starts at 2:50 pm and lasts 25 minutes.

5) Gail's games lesson starts at 11:40 am and lasts 1 hour 25 minutes.

6) Mara's maths lesson starts at 3:15 pm and lasts 55 minutes.

7) Malik's music lesson starts at 5:55 pm and lasts 90 minutes.

8) Dalia's dance lesson starts at 6:25 pm and lasts 110 minutes.

9) Dom's drama lesson starts at 6:50 pm and lasts 136 minutes.

10) Amy's art lesson starts at 3:17 pm and lasts 124 minutes.

Today I scored ☐ out of 10.

Week 4 — Day 3

Fill in the missing numbers in the sequence.

65, 69, 73, 77, 81, 85, 89

1) 93, 88, 83, ___ , ___ , ___ , ___

2) 113, 124, 135, ___ , ___ , ___ , ___

3) 45, 150, 255, ___ , ___ , ___ , ___

4) 884, 744, 604, ___ , ___ , ___ , ___

5) 297, 276, 255, ___ , ___ , ___ , ___

6) 365, 390, 415, ___ , ___ , ___ , ___

7) 799, 687, 575, ___ , ___ , ___ , ___

8) 443, 520, 597, ___ , ___ , ___ , ___

Today I scored ___ out of 8.

Week 4 — Day 4

Fill in the gaps in the number sentence.

$2^{\boxed{2}} = 2 \times 2 = \boxed{4}$

1) $\boxed{}^2 = 3 \times 3 = \boxed{}$

6) $4^{\boxed{}} = 4 \times 4 \times 4 = \boxed{}$

2) $2^{\boxed{}} = 2 \times 2 \times 2 = \boxed{}$

7) $\boxed{}^2 = \boxed{} \times \boxed{} = 1$

3) $5^{\boxed{}} = 5 \times 5 = \boxed{}$

8) $\boxed{}^2 = 121$

4) $\boxed{}^2 = \boxed{} \times \boxed{} = 16$

9) $\boxed{} = 6 \times 6 \times \boxed{} = 216$

5) $9^2 = \boxed{} \times \boxed{} = \boxed{}$

10) $10^3 = \boxed{}$

Today I scored $\boxed{}$ out of 10.

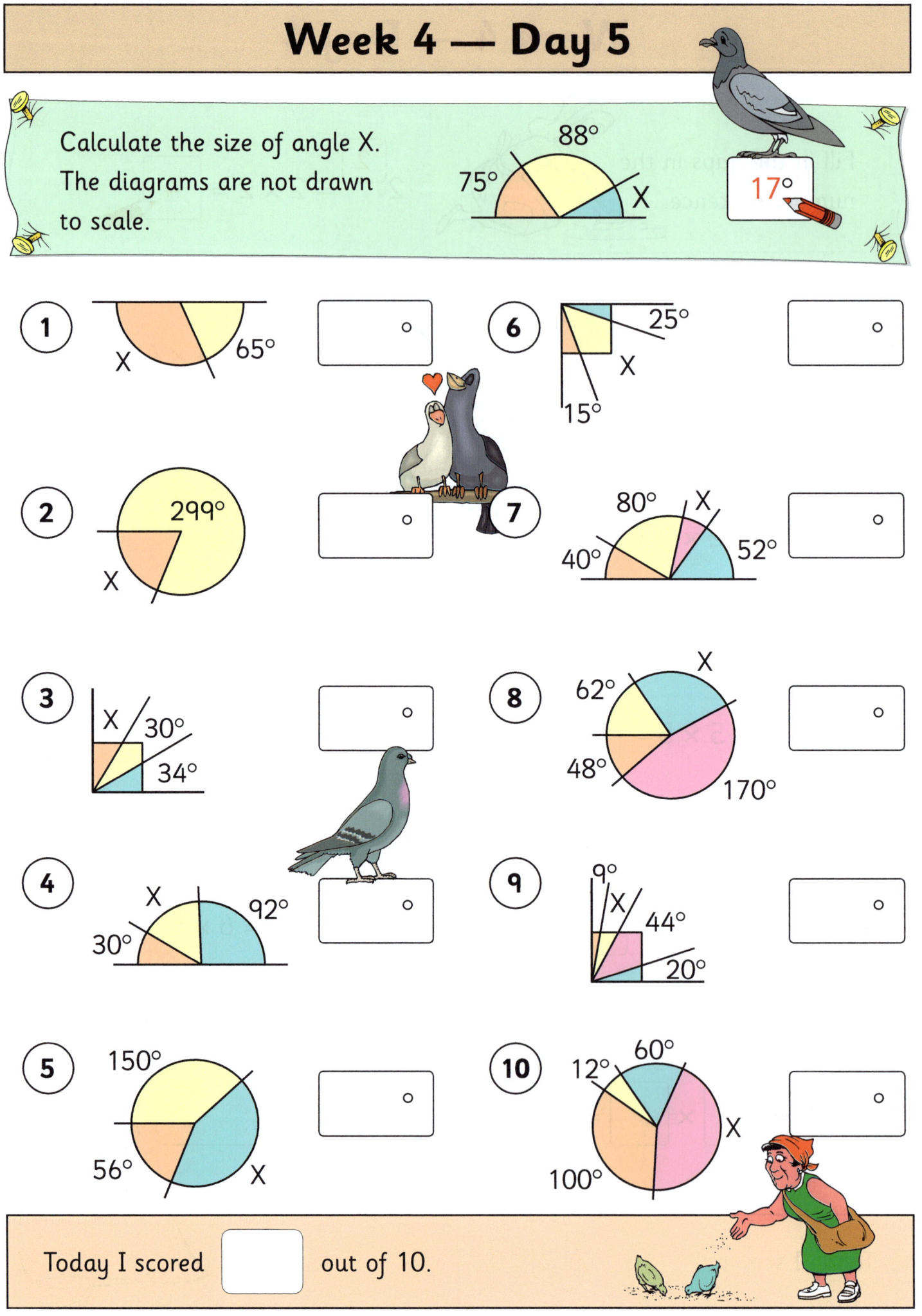

Week 5 — Day 1

Circle the calculation that gives the largest number. 3^2 ⬤5×2

1) 5^2 6×5

2) 4^2 3×5

3) 8×5 6^2

4) 6×8 7^2

5) 10^2 11×9

6) 7×10 8^2

7) 9^2 8×11

8) $2^2 \times 2$ 3^2

9) $3^2 \times 4$ $2^3 \times 3$

10) 3^3 7×2^2

11) 5×11 4^3

12) 11×12 5^3

Today I scored ☐ out of 12.

Week 5 — Day 2

Put a cross through the fraction that is not equivalent to the other two.

$\frac{1}{5}$ $\frac{2}{10}$ $\cancel{\frac{5}{15}}$

1) $\frac{2}{6}$ $\frac{2}{12}$ $\frac{1}{3}$

2) $\frac{5}{10}$ $\frac{25}{50}$ $\frac{2}{5}$

3) $\frac{25}{100}$ $\frac{10}{25}$ $\frac{1}{4}$

4) $\frac{16}{24}$ $\frac{3}{4}$ $\frac{12}{16}$

5) $\frac{1}{6}$ $\frac{3}{18}$ $\frac{6}{24}$

6) $\frac{16}{28}$ $\frac{21}{49}$ $\frac{3}{7}$

7) $\frac{16}{20}$ $\frac{45}{50}$ $\frac{9}{10}$

8) $\frac{5}{7}$ $\frac{35}{49}$ $\frac{44}{77}$

9) $\frac{20}{24}$ $\frac{25}{35}$ $\frac{5}{6}$

10) $\frac{2}{5}$ $\frac{5}{12}$ $\frac{25}{60}$

11) $\frac{3}{60}$ $\frac{3}{45}$ $\frac{1}{15}$

12) $\frac{150}{200}$ $\frac{3}{4}$ $\frac{100}{150}$

Today I scored ☐ out of 12.

Week 5 — Day 3

Write down the number of shoes.

A factory has made 10 000 shoes. $\frac{1}{5}$ of the shoes are red. How many shoes are not red?

8000

1) A factory has made 30 000 shoes. $\frac{2}{3}$ of the shoes have laces. How many shoes do not have laces?

2) A factory has made 50 000 shoes. $\frac{1}{5}$ of the shoes have high heels. How many shoes do not have high heels?

3) A factory has made 25 000 shoes. $\frac{2}{5}$ of the shoes are leather. How many shoes are not leather?

4) A factory has made 40 000 shoes. $\frac{1}{8}$ of the shoes are sandals. How many shoes are not sandals?

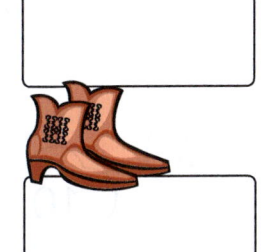

5) A factory has made 72 000 shoes. $\frac{7}{9}$ of the shoes are trainers. How many shoes are not trainers?

6) A factory has made 100 000 shoes. $\frac{15}{100}$ of the shoes have buckles. How many shoes do not have buckles?

7) A factory has made 84 000 shoes. $\frac{5}{12}$ of the shoes are waterproof. How many shoes are not waterproof?

8) A factory has made 42 000 shoes. $\frac{3}{7}$ of the shoes are black. How many shoes are not black?

Today I scored ☐ out of 8.

Week 5 — Day 4

Put a ring around all of the factors of the number in the cloud. Underline all of the multiples of the number in the cloud.

6 | ③ ② 56 | 36 70 18

1. **12** | 16 3 36 | 6 60 50

2. **9** | 43 3 27 | 6 72 2

3. **10** | 2 3 30 | 25 100 5

4. **8** | 4 18 6 | 2 72 56

5. **11** | 88 2 55 | 101 121 3

6. **14** | 29 2 140 | 70 7 3

7. **15** | 3 10 5 | 45 60 40

8. **20** | 50 4 6 | 10 80 5

9. **25** | 120 15 5 | 100 3 75

10. **60** | 20 5 12 | 3 100 120

11. **24** | 6 12 50 | 123 48 3

12. **100** | 400 3 75 | 250 25 5

Today I scored ☐ out of 12.

Week 5 — Day 5

How much time passed between the two points in time?

13:30, 12th May 2005
20:45, 30th May 2005

18 days, **7** hours, **15** minutes

1) 09:20, 14th April 2020
   11:55, 21st April 2020
   ☐ days, ☐ hours, ☐ minutes

2) 07:40, 13th July 2012
   21:45, 28th July 2012
   ☐ days, ☐ hours, ☐ minutes

3) 14:30, 20th June 2014
   22:30, 15th July 2014
   ☐ days, ☐ hours, ☐ minutes

4) 22:55, 12th April 2017
   23:45, 12th May 2017
   ☐ days, ☐ hours, ☐ minutes

5) 07:30, 2nd July 2009
   23:52, 9th August 2009
   ☐ days, ☐ hours, ☐ minutes

6) 06:18, 1st December 2018
   06:25, 1st January 2019
   ☐ days, ☐ hours, ☐ minutes

7) 10:30, 30th May 2000
   12:50, 15th June 2000
   ☐ days, ☐ hours, ☐ minutes

8) 14:50, 25th December 2019
   22:59, 1st January 2020
   ☐ days, ☐ hours, ☐ minutes

Today I scored ☐ out of 8.

Week 6 — Day 1

Complete the calculation.   3.2 × 100 = 320

1) 20 × 400 =

2) 5.2 × 10 =

3) 500 × 700 =

4) 10 × 0.87 =

5) 160 × 20 =

6) 0.45 × 100 =

7) 4.9 × 100 =

8) 80 × 90 =

9) 100 × 23.26 =

10) 1000 × 24.71 =

11) 1200 × 60 =

12) 793.4 × 1000 =

13) 120 × 120 =

14) 150 × 400 =

Today I scored ☐ out of 14.

Week 6 — Day 2

The graph shows how the temperature changed during the year. Fill in the sentences.

In November, it was **6** °C.

Between May and June the temperature increased by **2** °C.

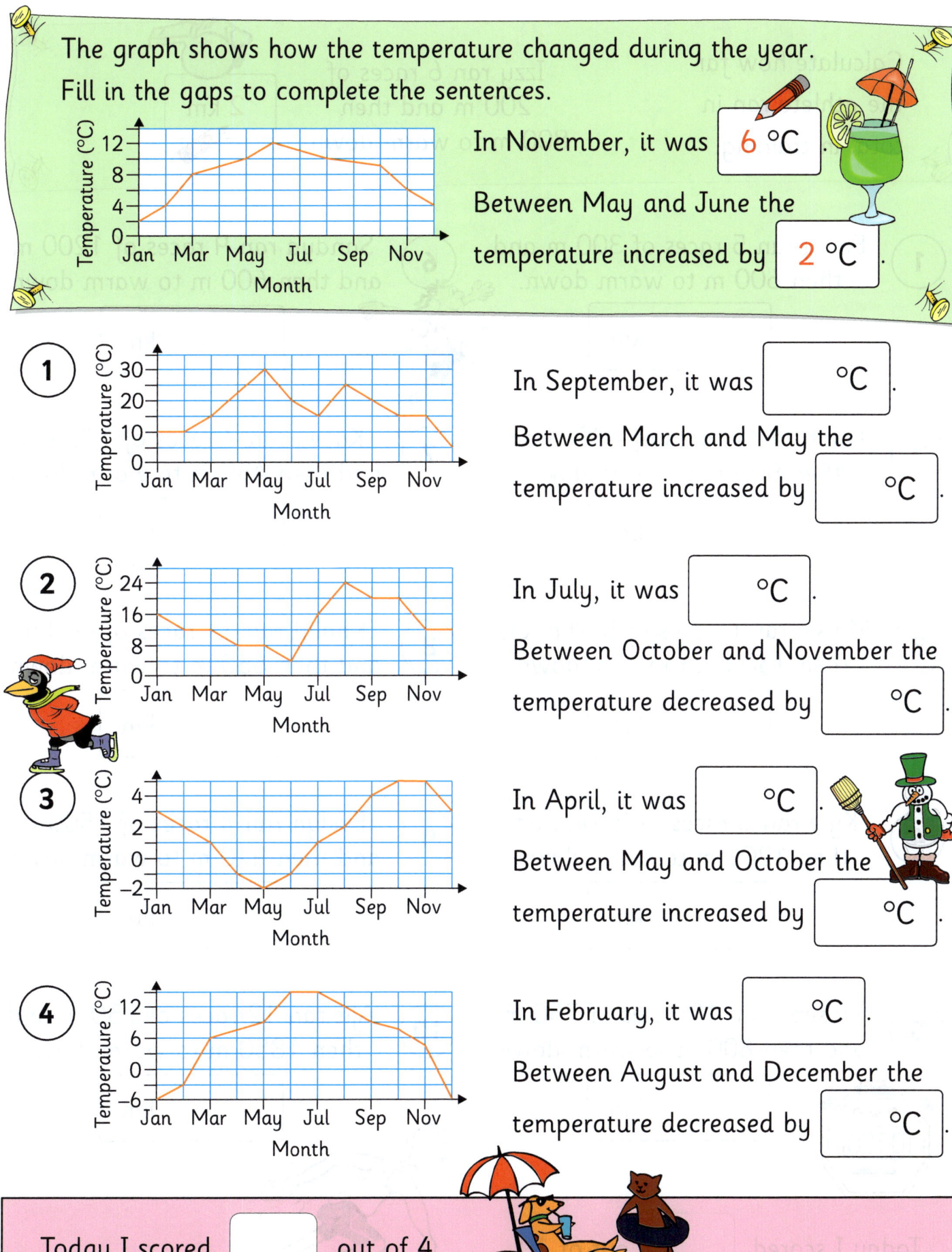

1 In September, it was ☐ °C.

Between March and May the temperature increased by ☐ °C.

2 In July, it was ☐ °C.

Between October and November the temperature decreased by ☐ °C.

3 In April, it was ☐ °C.

Between May and October the temperature increased by ☐ °C.

4 In February, it was ☐ °C.

Between August and December the temperature decreased by ☐ °C.

Today I scored ☐ out of 4.

Week 6 — Day 3

Calculate how far the athlete ran in total in training.

Izzy ran 6 races of 200 m and then 800 m to warm down.

2 km

1. Emily ran 5 races of 300 m and then 600 m to warm down.
   ____ km

2. Noah ran 4 races of 400 m and then 900 m to warm down.
   ____ km

3. Maisie ran 6 races of 500 m and then 1500 m to warm down.
   ____ km

4. Kyle ran 8 races of 900 m and then 1200 m to warm down.
   ____ km

5. Joseph ran 10 races of 750 m and then 800 m to warm down.
   ____ km

6. Sandya ran 9 races of 1200 m and then 600 m to warm down.
   ____ km

7. Kacey ran 7 races of 1100 m and then 450 m to warm down.
   ____ km

8. Khalid ran 11 races of 600 m and then 650 m to warm down.
   ____ km

9. Evelyn ran 4 races of 1500 m and then 920 m to warm down.
   ____ km

10. Ajit ran 12 races of 250 m and then 1850 m to warm down.
    ____ km

Today I scored ____ out of 10.

Week 6 — Day 4

Calculate the area of the shape. The shape is not drawn to scale.  = 2 cm²

18 cm²

1 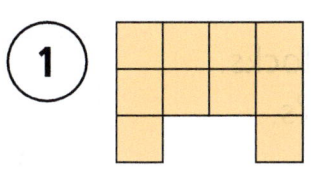 = 2 cm²

☐ cm²

5 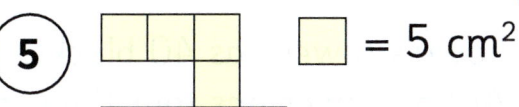 = 5 cm²

☐ cm²

2 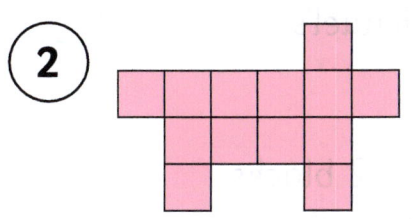 = 10 cm²

☐ cm²

6 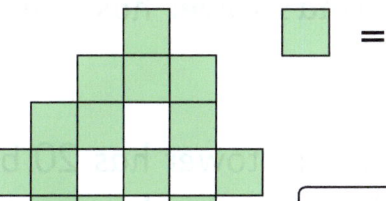 = 3 cm²

☐ cm²

3 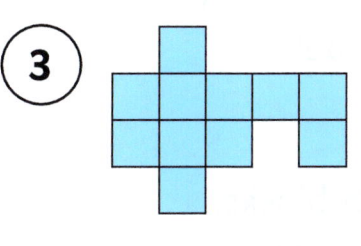 = 5 cm²

☐ cm²

7 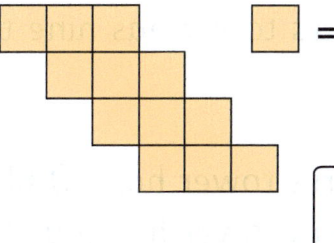 = 6 cm²

☐ cm²

4 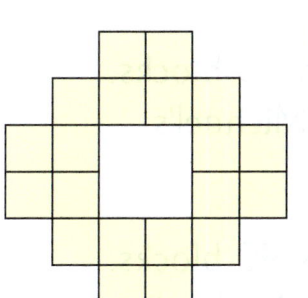 = 10 cm²

☐ cm²

8 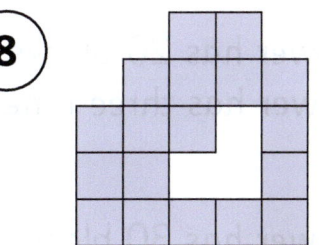 = 4 cm²

☐ cm²

Today I scored ☐ out of 8.

Week 6 — Day 5

How many times more blocks does Aisha's tower have compared to Lowri's?

Lowri's tower has 90 blocks. Michael's tower has 30 blocks. Aisha's tower has six times as many blocks as Michael's.

1) Lowri's tower has 40 blocks. Michael's tower has 20 blocks. Aisha's tower has four times as many blocks as Michael's.

2) Lowri's tower has 25 blocks. Michael's tower has 50 blocks. Aisha's tower has five times as many blocks as Michael's.

3) Lowri's tower has 20 blocks. Michael's tower has 12 blocks. Aisha's tower has ten times as many blocks as Michael's.

4) Lowri's tower has 120 blocks. Michael's tower has 40 blocks. Aisha's tower has nine times as many blocks as Michael's.

5) Lowri's tower has 10 blocks. Michael's tower has 15 blocks. Aisha's tower has four times as many blocks as Michael's.

6) Lowri's tower has 20 blocks. Michael's tower has 80 blocks. Aisha's tower has three times as many blocks as Michael's.

7) Lowri's tower has 30 blocks. Michael's tower has 90 blocks. Aisha's tower has eleven times as many blocks as Michael's.

Today I scored ☐ out of 7.

Week 7 — Day 1

Draw a ring around the shape that is a reflection of the shape in the box.

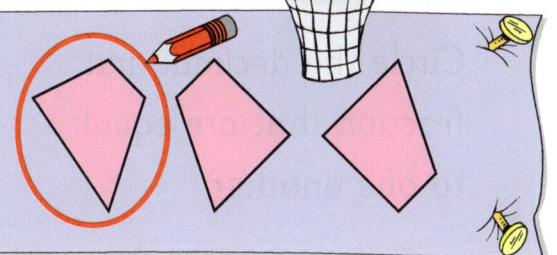

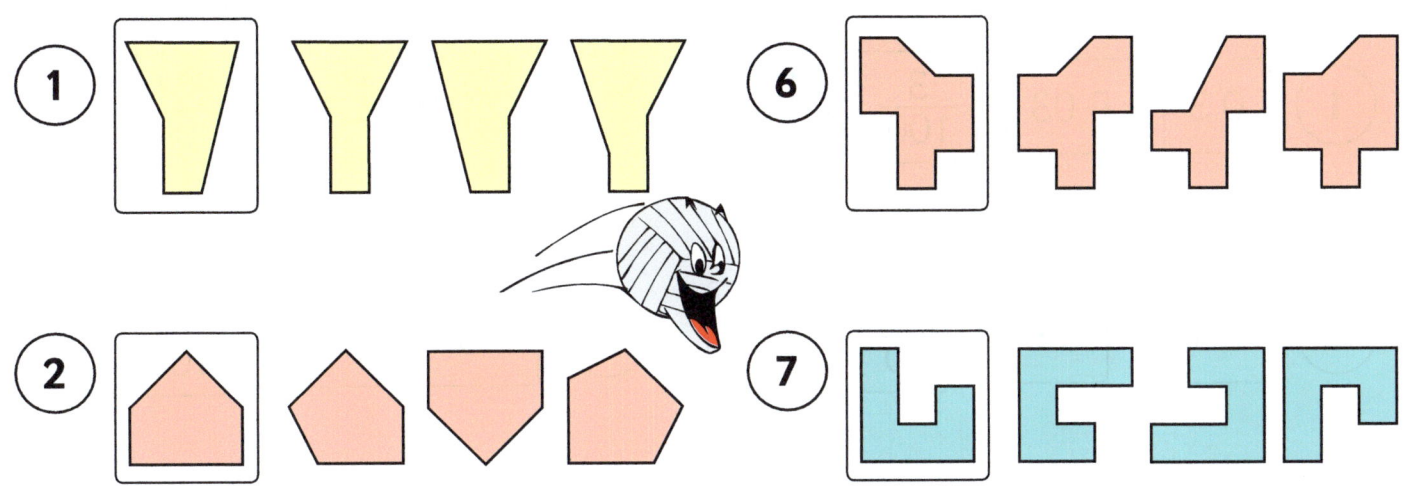

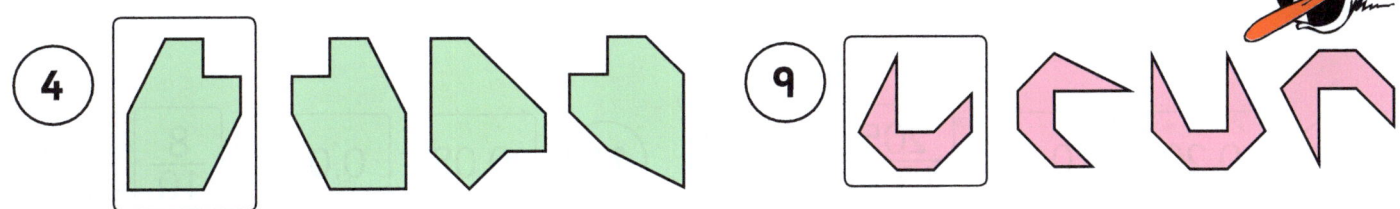

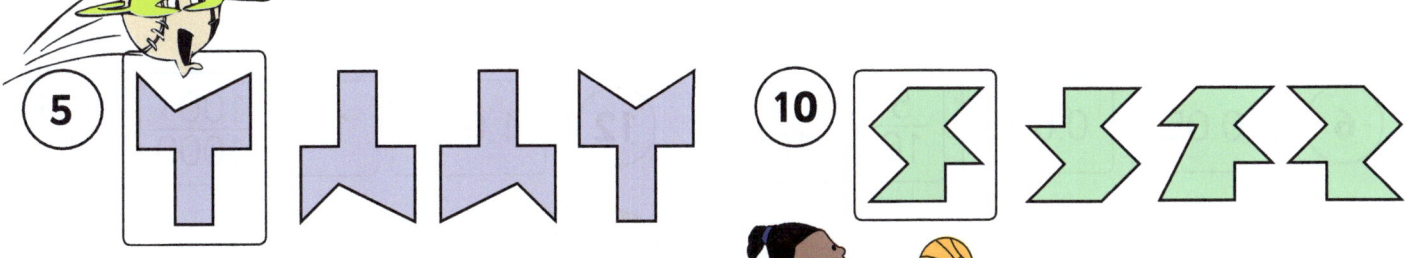

Today I scored ☐ out of 10.

Week 7 — Day 2

Circle the decimal and fraction that are equal to one another.

(0.2)   0.02   (20/100)   2/1000

1. 0.3   0.03   3/100   100/3
2. 0.16   0.61   16/10   16/100
3. 0.007   0.7   7/100   7/10
4. 0.455   4.55   455/1000   455/10
5. 0.205   0.25   205/1000   205/100
6. 0.05   0.005   5/10   5/100
7. 0.101   1.1   101/100   101/1000
8. 0.52   0.052   520/1000   520/100
9. 0.65   6.5   65/100   65/1000
10. 0.214   0.0214   214/1000   214/100
11. 0.08   0.008   8/10   8/1000
12. 1.001   1.1   1001/1000   101/1000

Today I scored [ ] out of 12.

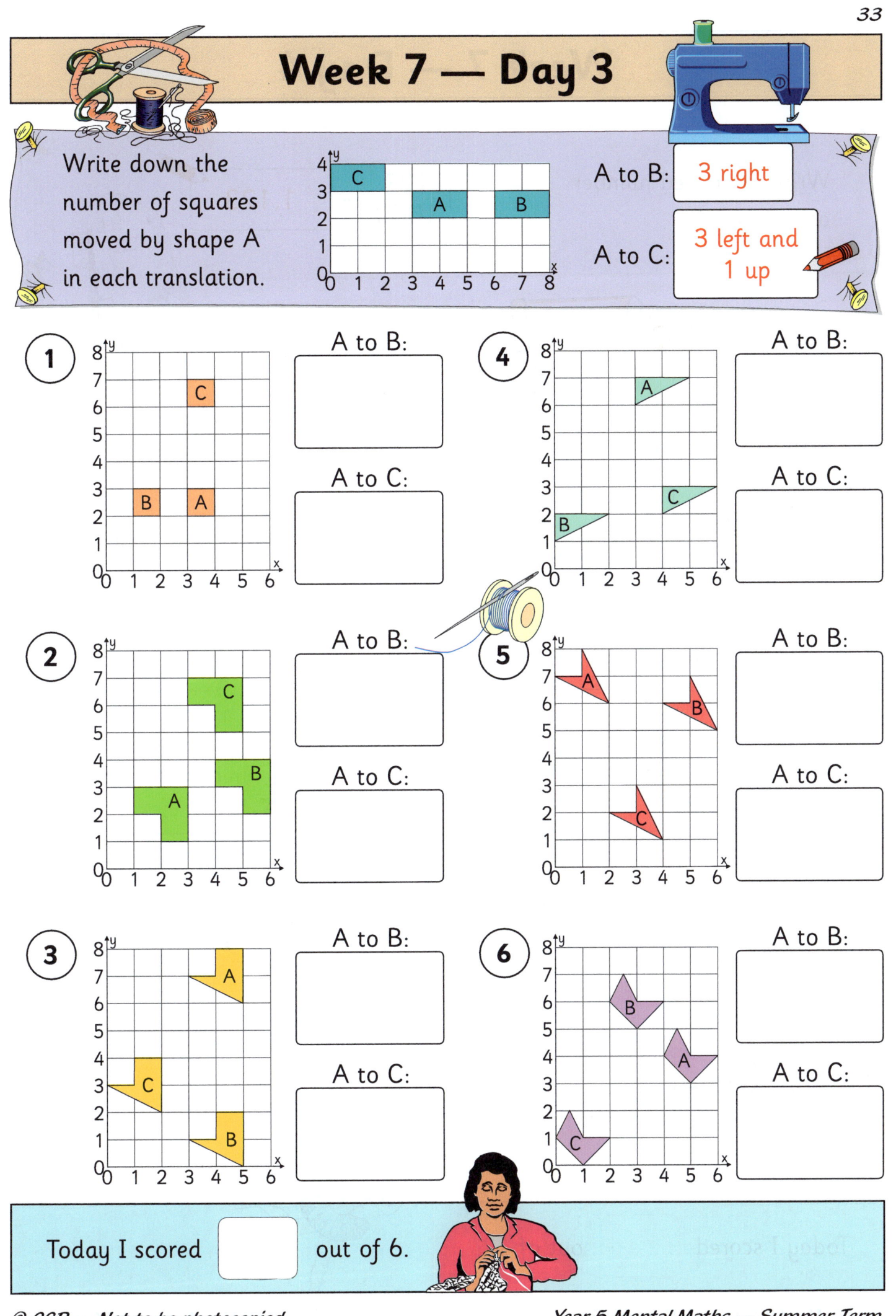

Week 7 — Day 4

Write the mixed number as a decimal.

$1\frac{123}{1000}$ = 1.123

1) $1\frac{614}{1000}$ =

2) $1\frac{211}{1000}$ =

3) $1\frac{595}{1000}$ =

4) $2\frac{341}{1000}$ =

5) $5\frac{500}{1000}$ =

6) $3\frac{78}{1000}$ =

7) $5\frac{640}{1000}$ =

8) $4\frac{14}{1000}$ =

9) $6\frac{5}{1000}$ =

10) $1\frac{2}{1000}$ =

11) $12\frac{980}{1000}$ =

12) $10\frac{400}{1000}$ =

Today I scored ☐ out of 12.

Week 7 — Day 5

The dashed line represents a mirror line. Write the coordinates of the reflections of points A and B.

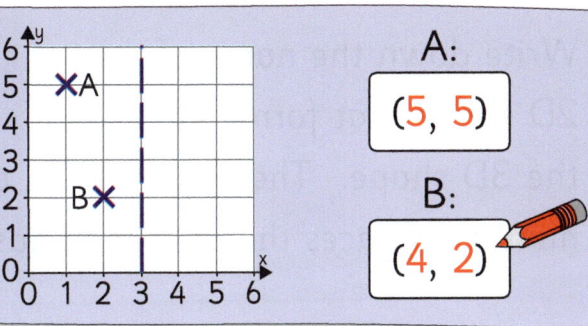

A: (5, 5)

B: (4, 2)

1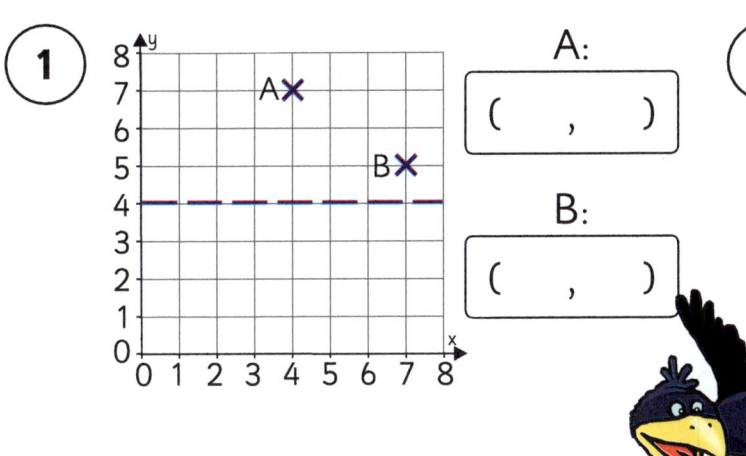

A: (,)

B: (,)

4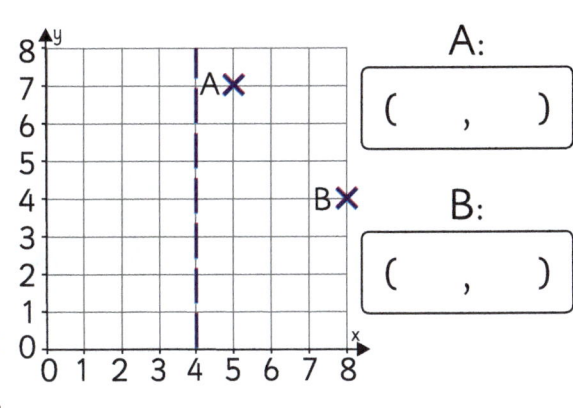

A: (,)

B: (,)

2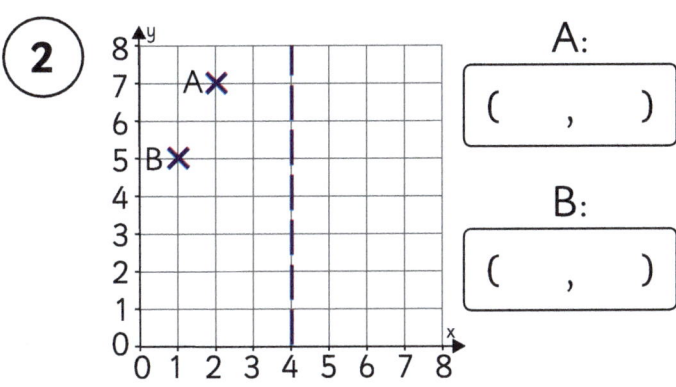

A: (,)

B: (,)

5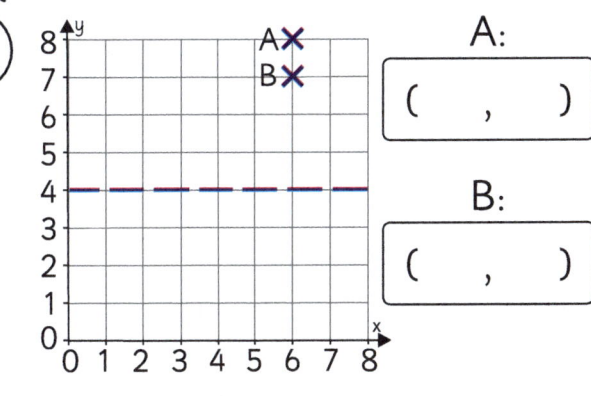

A: (,)

B: (,)

3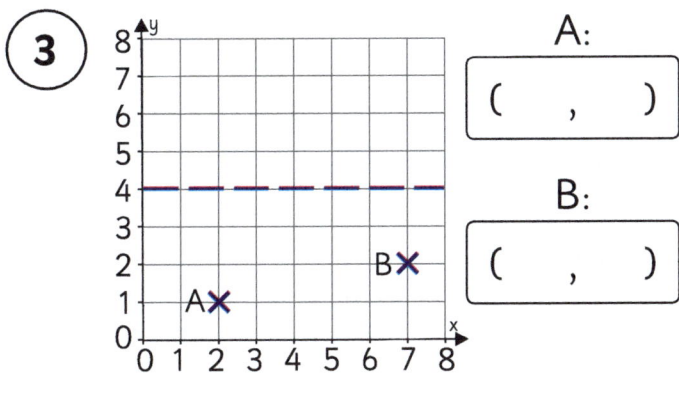

A: (,)

B: (,)

6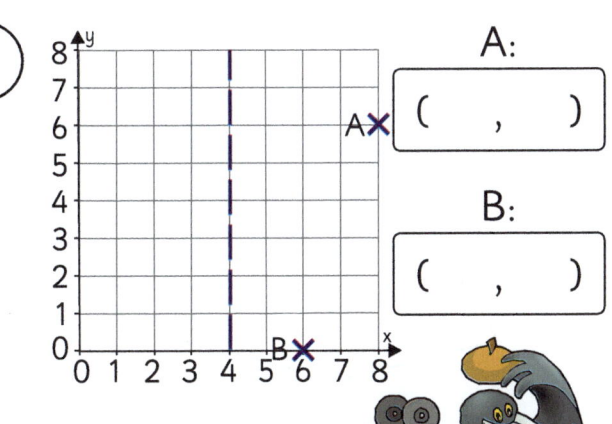

A: (,)

B: (,)

Today I scored [ ] out of 6.

Week 8 — Day 1

Write down the name of the 2D shape that forms the base of the 3D shape. Then write down the number of faces the 3D shape has.

square

6 faces

1. [rectangular prism] ☐ faces

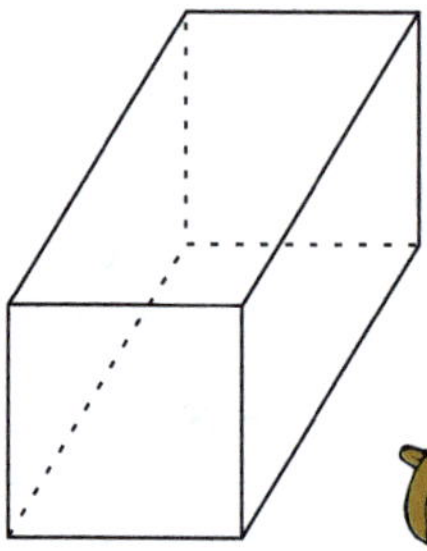

2. [cylinder] ☐ faces

3. [cone] ☐ faces

4. [square-based pyramid] ☐ faces

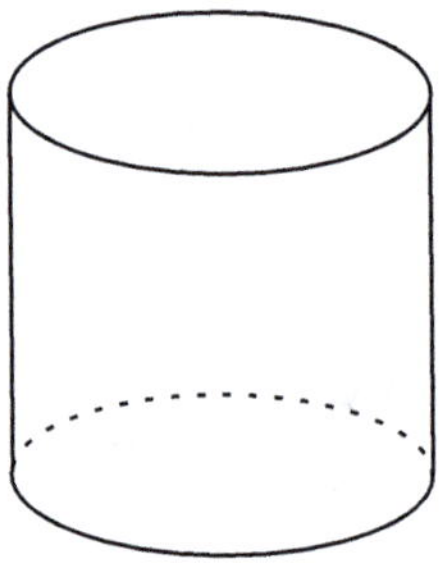

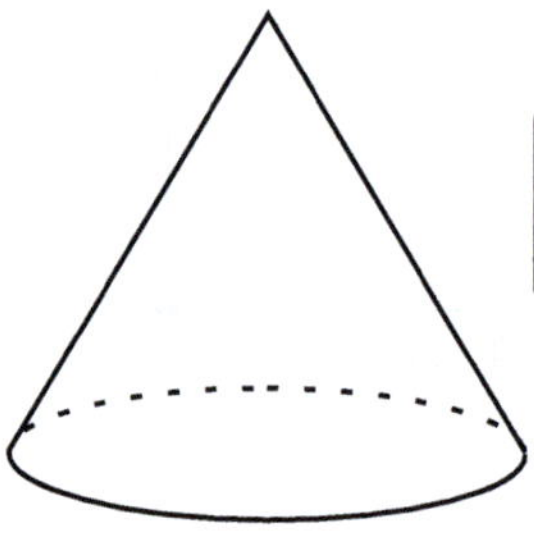

5. [triangular prism] ☐ faces

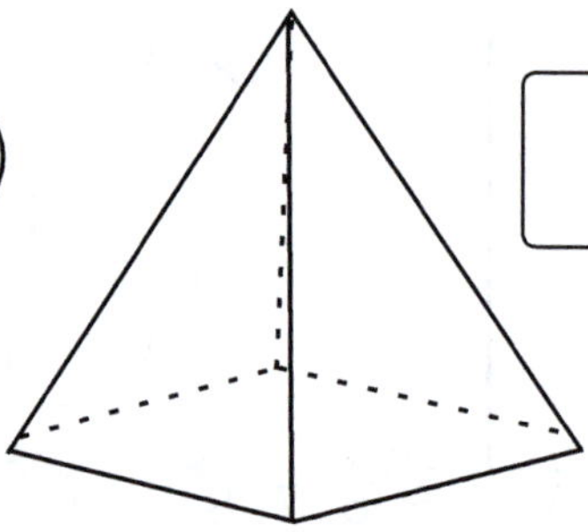

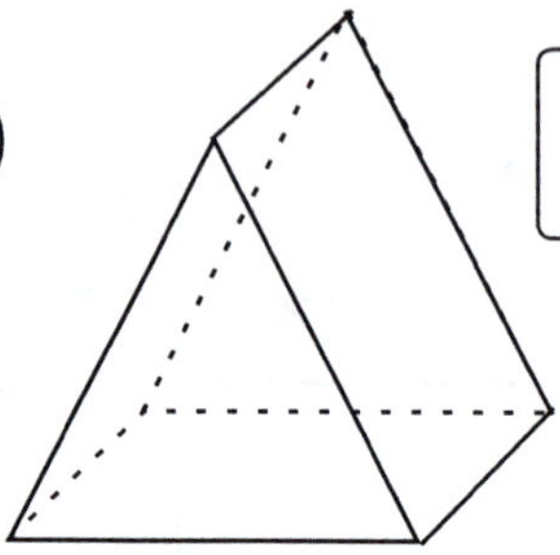

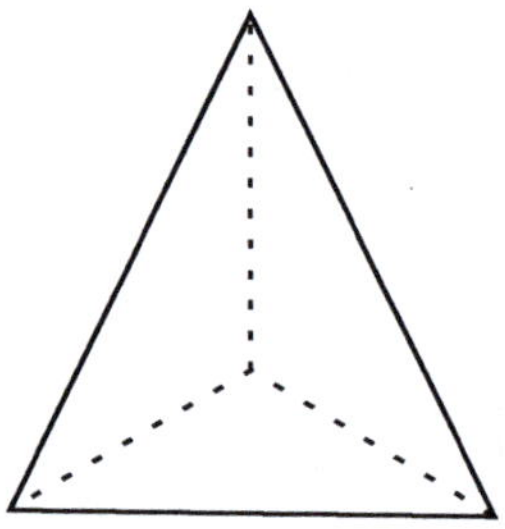

6. [tetrahedron] ☐ faces

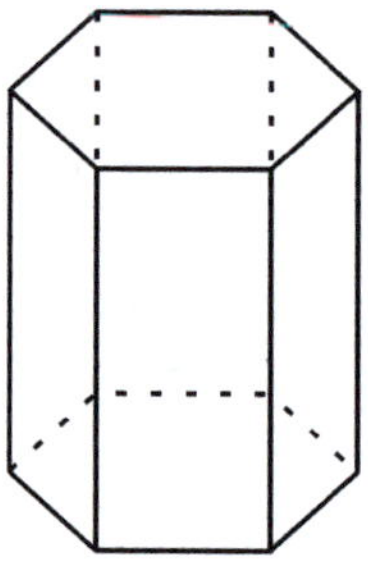

7. [hexagonal prism] ☐ faces

8. [pentagonal prism] ☐ faces

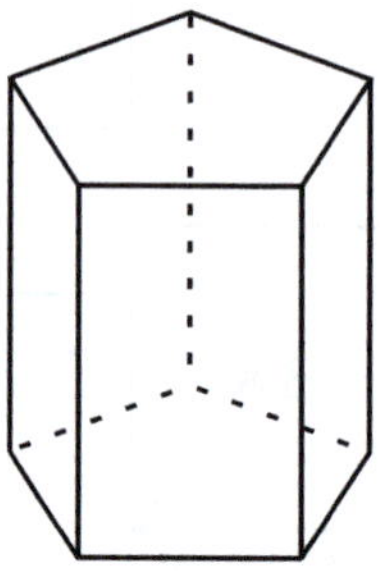

Today I scored ☐ out of 8.

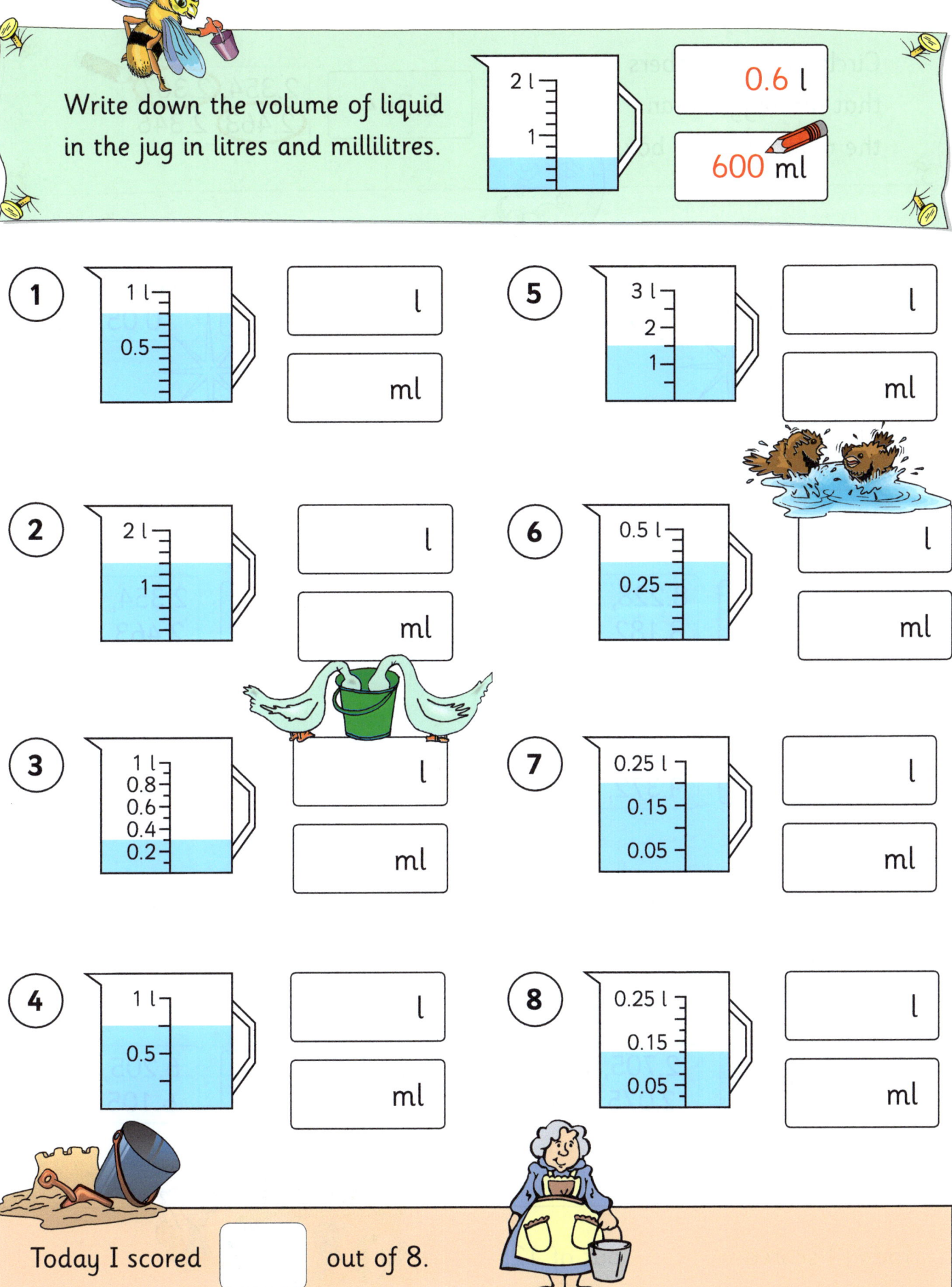

Week 8 — Day 3

Circle all the numbers that are bigger than the number in the box.

2.364   2.354, ⊙2.367⊙, ⊙2.463⊙, 2.346

1. 1.832 — 1.843, 1.833, 2.238, 1.283
2. 5.645 — 5.456, 5.546, 5.654, 5.564
3. 8.282 — 8.228, 8.822, 8.182, 8.283
4. 9.473 — 9.374, 9.347, 9.372, 9.482
5. 7.012 — 7.021, 7.022, 7.002, 7.21
6. 2.507 — 2.705, 2.75, 2.075, 2.57
7. 0.005 — 0.004, 0.006, 0.05, 0.6
8. 6.59 — 6.409, 6.508, 6.95, 6.592
9. 2.364 — 2.354, 2.367, 2.463, 2.346
10. 4.2 — 4.22, 4.02, 4.002, 4.202
11. 9.789 — 9.879, 9.788, 9.799, 9.798
12. 6.501 — 6.205, 6.51, 6.105, 6.15

Today I scored ☐ out of 12.

Year 5 Mental Maths — Summer Term

Week 8 — Day 4

A machine used to cut planks of wood sometimes cuts them too short or too long. Calculate the actual length of the cut plank.

The plank should have been 24 m, but the machine cut it 2 cm too short.

Actual length: 23.98 m

1. The plank should have been 7.5 m, but the machine cut it 5 cm too long.

   Actual length: ___ m

2. The plank should have been 546 cm, but the machine cut it 3 mm too short.

   Actual length: ___ cm

3. The plank should have been 2.5 m, but the machine cut it 4 mm too long.

   Actual length: ___ m

4. The plank should have been 3.12 m, but the machine cut it 7 mm too short.

   Actual length: ___ m

5. The plank should have been 4.98 m, but the machine cut it 6 mm too short.

   Actual length: ___ m

6. The plank should have been 8.9 m, but the machine cut it 0.5 cm too long.

   Actual length: ___ m

Today I scored ___ out of 6.

Week 8 — Day 5

| | How much drink is there in each glass? | Judy has 6 l of lemonade. She pours half of it into a jug and divides the rest equally between 6 glasses. | 0.5 l |

1. John has 2 l of mango juice. He pours half of it into a jug and divides the rest equally between 5 glasses. _____ l

2. Jade has 3 l of lemonade. She pours one third of it into a jug and divides the rest equally between 8 glasses. _____ l

3. Jess has 4 l of fizzy pop. She pours one quarter of it into a jug and divides the rest equally between 6 glasses. _____ l

4. Ji has 6 l of blackcurrant squash. She pours two thirds of it into a jug and divides the rest equally between 10 glasses. _____ l

5. Jasper has 2 l of apple juice. He pours two fifths of it into a jug and divides the rest equally between 4 glasses. _____ l

6. Jordan has 1.5 l of milk. She pours one fifth of it into a jug and divides the rest equally between 6 glasses. _____ l

7. Jack has 0.8 l of water. He pours three quarters of it into a jug and divides the rest equally between 2 glasses. _____ l

8. Jamal has 14 l of orange juice. He pours two sevenths of it into a jug and divides the rest equally between 20 glasses. _____ l

9. Jared has 2.5 l of ginger beer. He pours three fifths of it into a jug and divides the rest equally between 10 glasses. _____ l

Today I scored _____ out of 9.

Year 5 Mental Maths — Summer Term

Week 9 — Day 1

Write the fraction as a percentage.

$\frac{1}{2}$ = 50%

1) $\frac{1}{4}$ = ☐ %

2) $\frac{60}{100}$ = ☐ %

3) $\frac{1}{10}$ = ☐ %

4) $\frac{5}{100}$ = ☐ %

5) $\frac{1}{5}$ = ☐ %

6) $\frac{100}{100}$ = ☐ %

7) $\frac{2}{5}$ = ☐ %

8) $\frac{8}{10}$ = ☐ %

9) $\frac{4}{5}$ = ☐ %

10) $\frac{25}{50}$ = ☐ %

11) $\frac{40}{50}$ = ☐ %

12) $\frac{1}{25}$ = ☐ %

Today I scored ☐ out of 12.

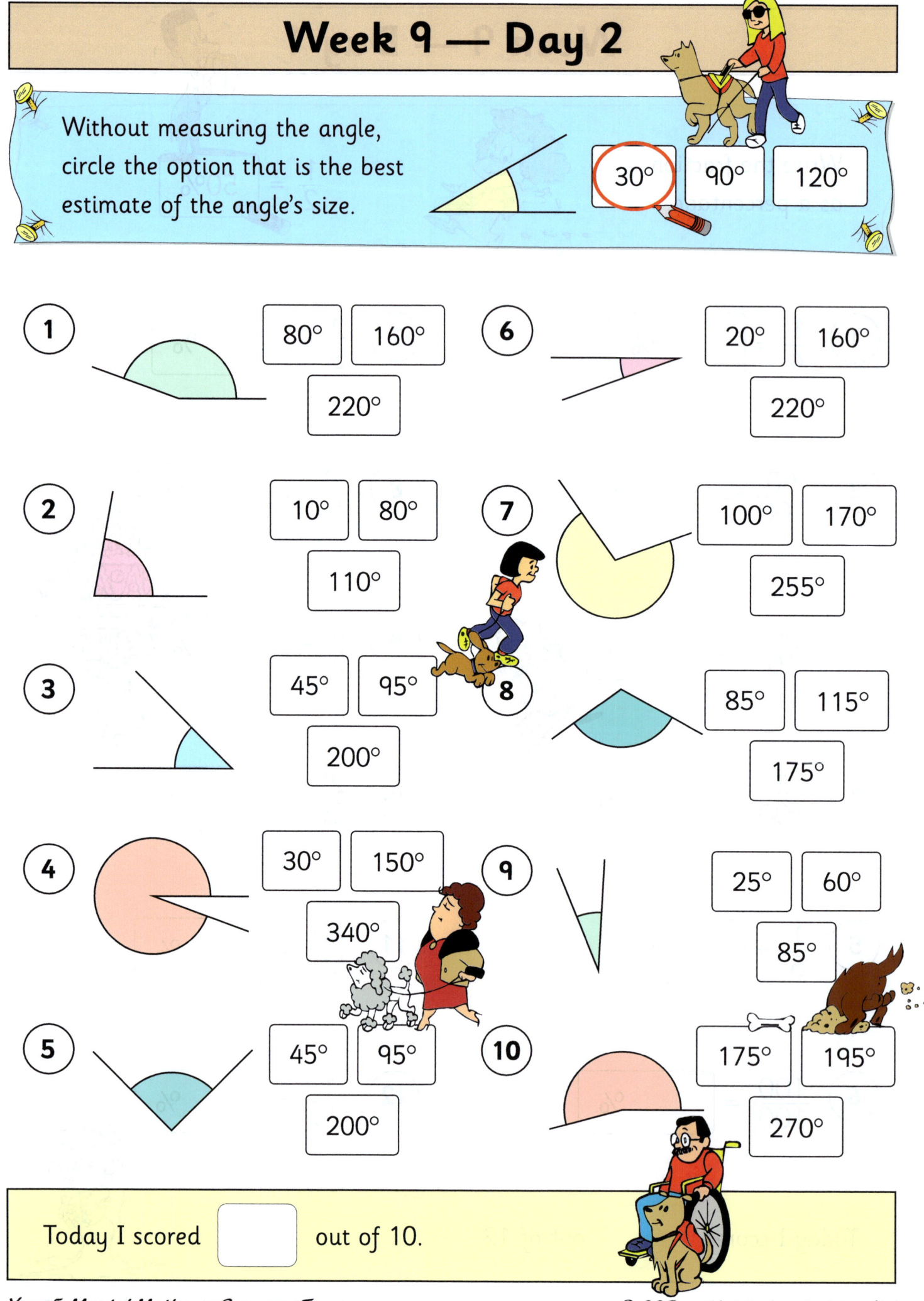

Week 9 — Day 3

A school has voted for a new school council. Write down the percentage of the total pupils that voted for the given pupil.

100 pupils voted in total. 11 pupils voted for Huw.

11%

1. 100 pupils voted in total. 43 pupils voted for Ella.
   ___ %

2. 100 pupils voted in total. 20 pupils voted for Isla.
   ___ %

3. 50 pupils voted in total. 15 pupils voted for Michael.
   ___ %

4. 50 pupils voted in total. 6 pupils voted for Eric.
   ___ %

5. 200 pupils voted in total. 30 pupils voted for Ore.
   ___ %

6. 200 pupils voted in total. 42 pupils voted for Arwa.
   ___ %

7. 50 pupils voted in total. 16 pupils voted for Morgan.
   ___ %

8. 200 pupils voted in total. 96 pupils voted for Kim.
   ___ %

9. 50 pupils voted in total. 47 pupils voted for Róisín.
   ___ %

10. 200 pupils voted in total. 174 pupils voted for Colin.
    ___ %

Today I scored ___ out of 10.

Week 9 — Day 4

The table gives information about a block of flats. Every flat in the block is identical. Work out the missing number.

Number of flats	150
Number of bathrooms	450
Number of bedrooms	600

In two flats, there are **6** bathrooms.

1)
Number of flats	200
Number of bathrooms	400
Number of bedrooms	600

In one flat, there are ☐ bathrooms.

2)
Number of flats	25
Number of bathrooms	25
Number of bedrooms	75

In one flat, there are ☐ bedrooms.

3)
Number of flats	15
Number of bathrooms	60
Number of bedrooms	75

In two flats, there are ☐ bathrooms.

4)
Number of flats	160
Number of bathrooms	320
Number of bedrooms	800

In three flats, there are ☐ bedrooms.

5)
Number of flats	120
Number of bathrooms	480
Number of bedrooms	600

In two flats, there are ☐ bathrooms.

6)
Number of flats	75
Number of bathrooms	75
Number of bedrooms	225

In six flats, there are ☐ bedrooms.

7)
Number of flats	175
Number of bathrooms	350
Number of bedrooms	700

In two flats, there are ☐ bedrooms.

8)
Number of flats	225
Number of bathrooms	675
Number of bedrooms	900

In three flats, there are ☐ bathrooms.

Today I scored ☐ out of 8.

Week 9 — Day 5

Put the values in order, from smallest to largest.

| 0.12 | $\frac{16}{100}$ | 15% |

| 0.12 | 15% | $\frac{16}{100}$ |

1) 0.45   40% $\frac{50}{100}$

2) $\frac{55}{100}$ 0.5   5%

3) 66% $\frac{6}{10}$ 0.63

4) $\frac{1}{4}$ 27%   0.2

5) 0.8 $\frac{15}{20}$ 70%

6) $\frac{2}{5}$ 0.3   45%

7) 90%   0.85 $\frac{40}{50}$

8) 36% $\frac{10}{25}$ 0.39

Today I scored ☐ out of 8.

Week 10 — Day 1

Find the length marked X and the angle marked Y. If there are two Xs or Ys marked, the lengths or angles are the same. The rectangles are not drawn to scale.

Perimeter = 21 cm — 18°, Y, 32°, X, 5.5 cm → 5 cm, 40°

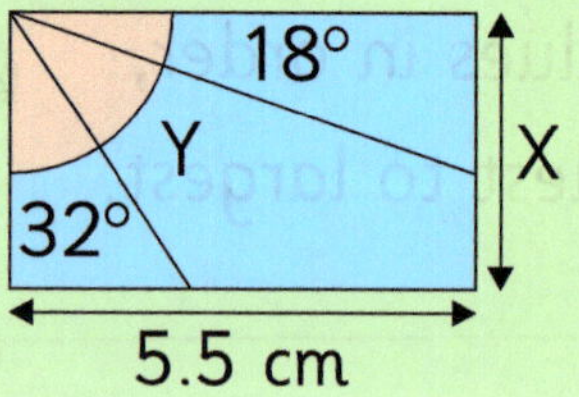

1) 4 cm, 50°, Y, X — ___ cm, ___°

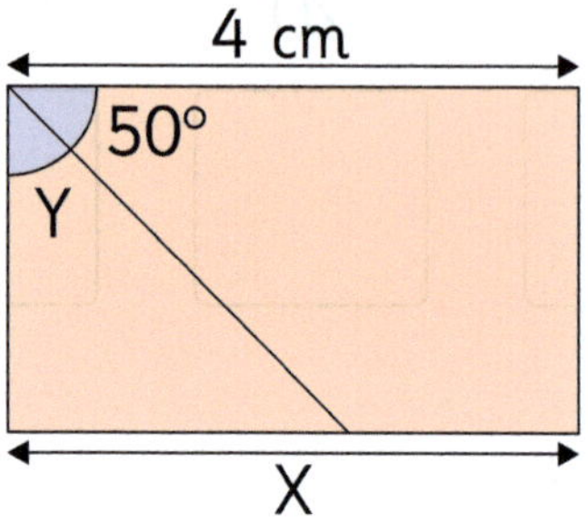

2) Perimeter = 9 cm, 19°, Y, 51°, X, 2.5 cm — ___ cm, ___°

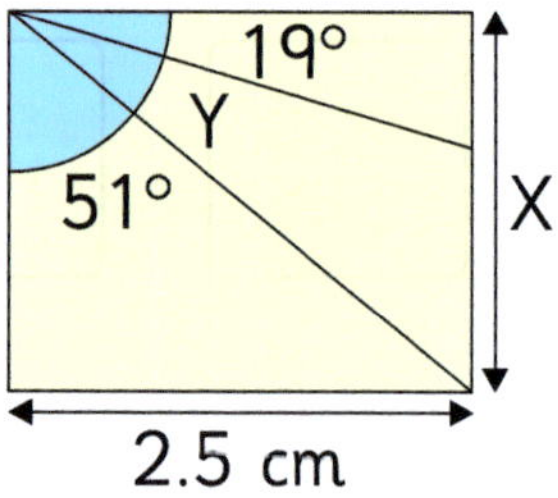

3) Perimeter = 24 cm, X, Y — ___ cm, ___°

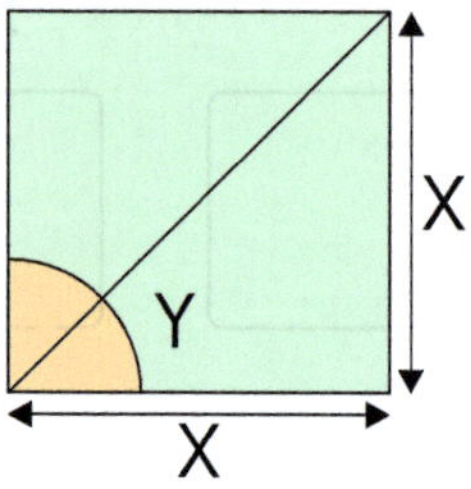

4) Perimeter = 39 cm, 38°, Y, X, 11 cm — ___ cm, ___°

5) Perimeter = 67 cm, 64°, Y, 51°, X, 15 cm — ___ cm, ___°

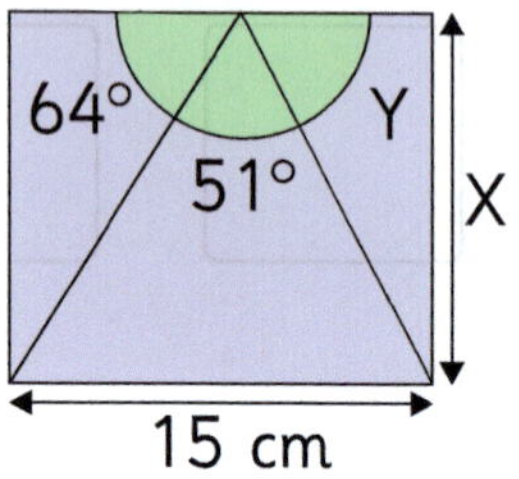

6) Perimeter = 6.84 m, Y, 57°, 57°, 1.2 m, X — ___ m, ___°

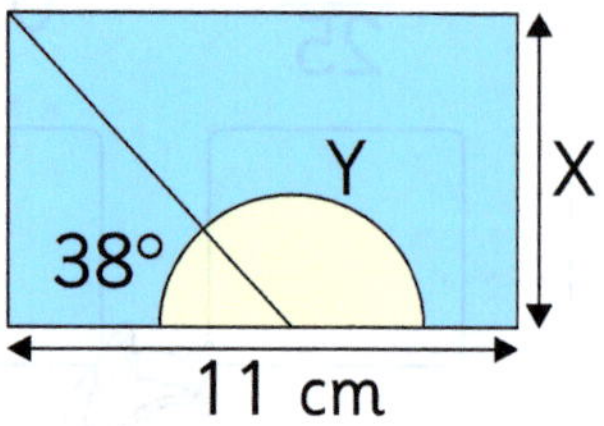

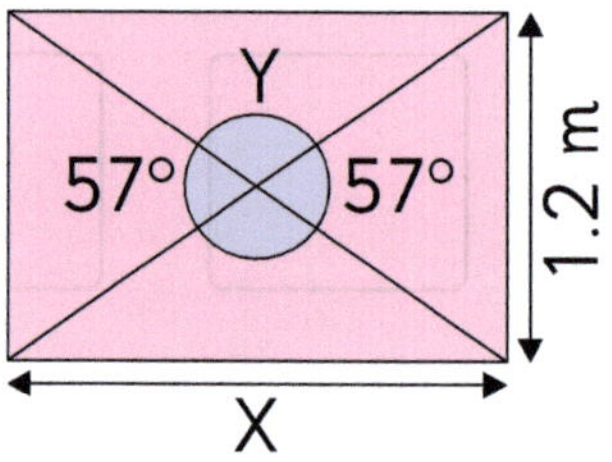

7) Perimeter = 10.38 m, 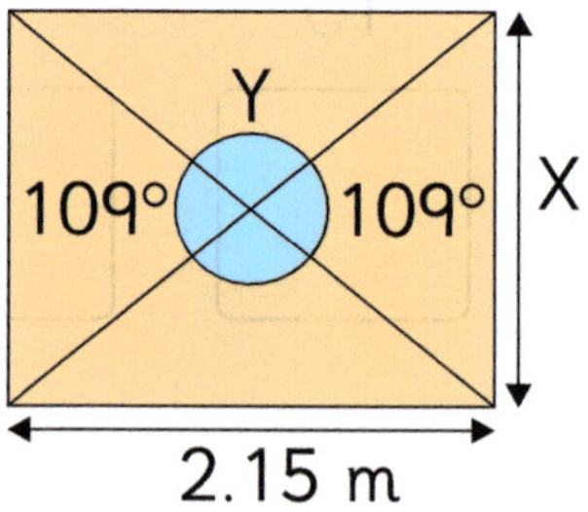 Y, 109°, 109°, X, 2.15 m — ___ m, ___°

8) Perimeter = 9.5 m, X, Y, 3.05 m — ___ m, ___°

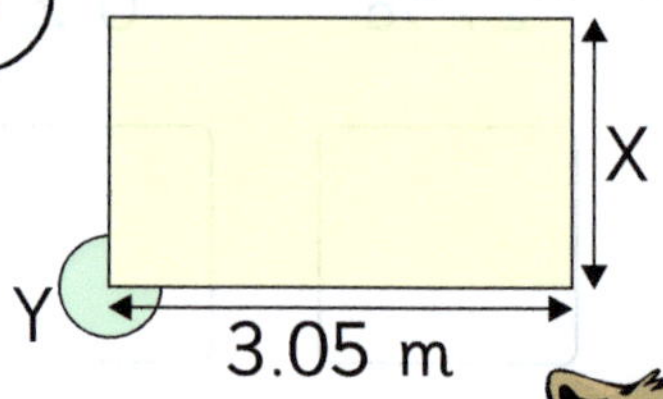

Today I scored ___ out of 8.

Year 5 Mental Maths — Summer Term © CGP — Not to be photocopied

Week 10 — Day 2

Write the number in the balloon to the nearest whole number in the first box and to one decimal place in the second box.

14.37 → 14 / 14.4

1. 3.48
2. 6.63
3. 12.89
4. 21.54
5. 78.65
6. 102.09
7. 230.99
8. 673.95

Today I scored ☐ out of 8.

Week 10 — Day 3

2.5 cm is approximately 1 inch.
There are 12 inches in 1 foot.
Convert the length of the item.

35 cm → **1** ft **2** in

1) 7.5 cm → ___ in

2) 8 ft 4 in → ___ cm

3) 5 ft → ___ cm

4) 18 in → ___ cm

5) 150 cm → ___ ft ___ in

6) 125 cm → ___ ft ___ in

7) 9 ft 2 in → ___ cm

8) 350 cm → ___ ft ___ in

9) 0.2 in → ___ cm

10) 30 m → ___ ft ___ in

Today I scored ___ out of 10.

Week 10 — Day 4

Work out the answer. Write your answer as a mixed number if possible.

$\frac{2}{7} + \frac{16}{21} = \boxed{1\frac{1}{21}}$

1) $\frac{1}{3} + \frac{1}{3} =$

2) $\frac{4}{5} - \frac{2}{5} =$

3) $\frac{1}{4} + \frac{3}{8} =$

4) $\frac{9}{10} - \frac{1}{5} =$

5) $\frac{2}{3} + \frac{3}{6} =$

6) $\frac{4}{12} - \frac{1}{4} =$

7) $\frac{4}{5} + \frac{9}{15} =$

8) $\frac{7}{9} - \frac{7}{18} =$

9) $\frac{22}{24} + \frac{5}{8} =$

10) $\frac{9}{15} - \frac{11}{30} =$

11) $\frac{42}{60} + \frac{7}{20} =$

12) $\frac{16}{25} - \frac{13}{100} =$

13) $\frac{51}{56} + \frac{3}{7} =$

14) $\frac{8}{9} - \frac{5}{108} =$

Today I scored ☐ out of 14.

Week 10 — Day 5

Fill in the missing number to complete the sentence about the Island of Rayshio.

25% of dogs are called Rover. This means that 1 out of every **4** dogs is called Rover.

1. 10% of cats are tabby. This means that 1 out of every ☐ cats is tabby.

2. 20% of people have curly hair. This means that 1 out of every ☐ people has curly hair.

3. 9 out of every 50 goats have beards. This means that ☐ % of goats have beards.

4. 12 out of every 25 people have freckles. This means that ☐ % of people have freckles.

5. 40% of fish are tropical. This means that ☐ out of every 5 fish are tropical.

6. 75% of people like bananas. This means that ☐ out of every 4 people like bananas.

7. 3 out of every 20 cars are grey. This means that ☐ % of cars are grey.

8. 60% of parrots have escaped. This means that ☐ out of every 10 parrots have escaped.

9. 38 out of every 200 days are sunny. This means that ☐ % of days are sunny.

10. 450 out of every 500 houses are brick. This means that ☐ % of houses are brick.

Today I scored ☐ out of 10.

Week 11 — Day 1

Circle the number that is the best estimate for the calculation in the box.

59.6 ÷ 2.8 → 12 / **20** / 30

1) 3.9 × 6.2 → 18 / 24 / 28

2) 34.7 ÷ 5.1 → 5 / 7 / 8

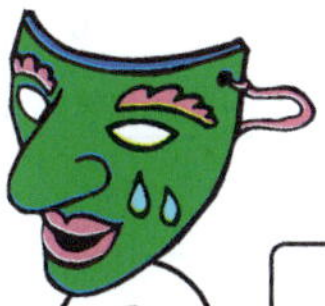

3) 6.85 × 11.24 → 60 / 66 / 77

4) 178 ÷ 3.11 → 60 / 90 / 120

5) 24.71 × 3.83 → 75 / 100 / 125

6) 148.5 ÷ 4.76 → 30 / 50 / 70

7) 203 × 8.2 → 1600 / 1800 / 2000

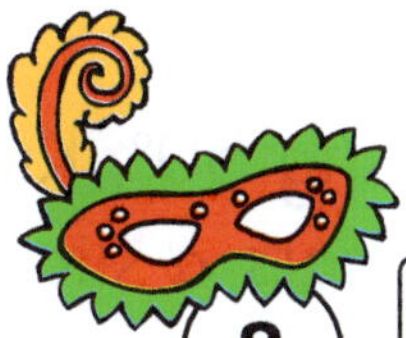

8) 8112 ÷ 901.8 → 9 / 90 / 900

9) 50.86 × 48.2 → 1500 / 2000 / 2500

10) 3989 ÷ 49.1 → 50 / 60 / 80

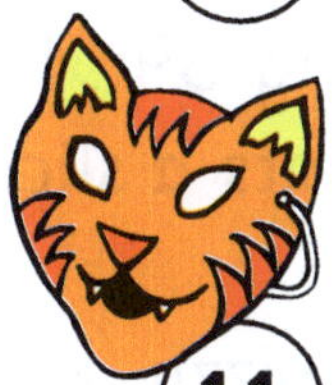

11) 126.1 × 4.05 → 300 / 400 / 500

12) 5610 ÷ 78.52 → 50 / 70 / 80

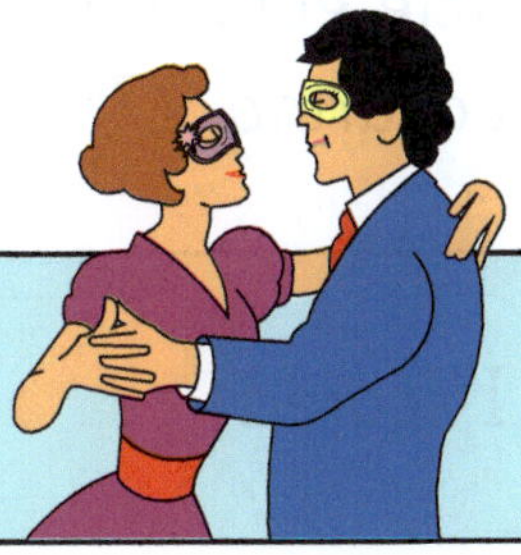

Today I scored ☐ out of 12.

Week 11 — Day 2

Some friends share a pizza. Calculate how much pizza has been eaten in degrees.

Lucie eats half of the pizza, Kwame eats a slice measuring 20° and Kai eats a slice measuring 60°.

260°

1. Lucie eats a quarter of the pizza, Kwame eats half of the pizza and Kai eats a slice measuring 47°.

2. Lucie eats a slice measuring 50°, Kwame eats a quarter of the pizza and Kai eats a slice measuring 55°.

3. Lucie eats three quarters of the pizza, Kwame eats a slice measuring 32° and Kai eats a slice measuring 36°.

4. Lucie eats a slice measuring 110°, Kwame eats a slice measuring 65° and Kai eats a slice measuring 95°.

5. Lucie eats a slice measuring 37°, Kwame eats a slice measuring 83° and Kai eats a slice measuring 95°.

6. Lucie eats a slice measuring 39°, Kwame eats a slice measuring 97° and Kai eats a slice measuring 63°.

7. Lucie eats a third of the pizza, Kwame eats a slice measuring 154° and Kai eats a slice measuring 45°.

8. Lucie eats a slice measuring 92°, Kwame eats a sixth of the pizza and Kai eats a slice measuring 94°.

9. Lucie eats a ninth of the pizza, Kwame eats a slice measuring 27° and Kai eats a slice measuring 105°.

Today I scored ☐ out of 9.

Year 5 Mental Maths — Summer Term

Week 11 — Day 3

Convert the amount of time into the units given in the answer box.

$2\frac{1}{2}$ hours → **150** minutes

1) $1\frac{1}{6}$ hours → ____ minutes

2) $\frac{2}{5}$ of an hour → ____ minutes

3) $2\frac{1}{3}$ hours → ____ minutes

4) $2\frac{1}{2}$ days → ____ hours

5) $1\frac{3}{4}$ days → ____ hours

6) $10\frac{1}{3}$ days → ____ hours

7) $\frac{12}{20}$ of an hour → ____ minutes

8) $6\frac{2}{3}$ hours → ____ minutes

9) $3\frac{5}{6}$ hours → ____ minutes

10) $3\frac{7}{12}$ days → ____ hours

Today I scored ____ out of 10.

Week 11 — Day 4

Circle the option that gives the same answer as the calculation in the yellow box.

2^2	(20 ÷ 5)	10 ÷ 2	2 × 4

1. 4^2 | 6 × 3 | 4 × 2 | 32 ÷ 2 | 30 ÷ 2

2. 2^3 | 64 ÷ 8 | 32 ÷ 2 | 3 × 4 | 24 ÷ 4

3. 6^2 | 66 ÷ 11 | 96 ÷ 8 | 4 × 9 | 90 ÷ 3

4. 3^3 | 90 ÷ 10 | 9 × 9 | 6 × 9 | 9 × 3

5. $1^3 + 5^2$ | 7 × 4 | 100 ÷ 4 | 13 × 2 | 14 × 2

6. 4^3 | 60 ÷ 5 | 4 × 16 | 4 × 9 | 3 × 4

7. $10^2 + 21$ | 82 ÷ 2 | 7 × 30 | 11 × 12 | 11^2

8. $7^2 + 3^2$ | 29 × 2 | 60 ÷ 3 | 25 × 4 | 42 ÷ 2

9. 10^3 | 50 × 2 | 500 × 2 | 20 × 5 | 250 × 2

Today I scored ☐ out of 9.

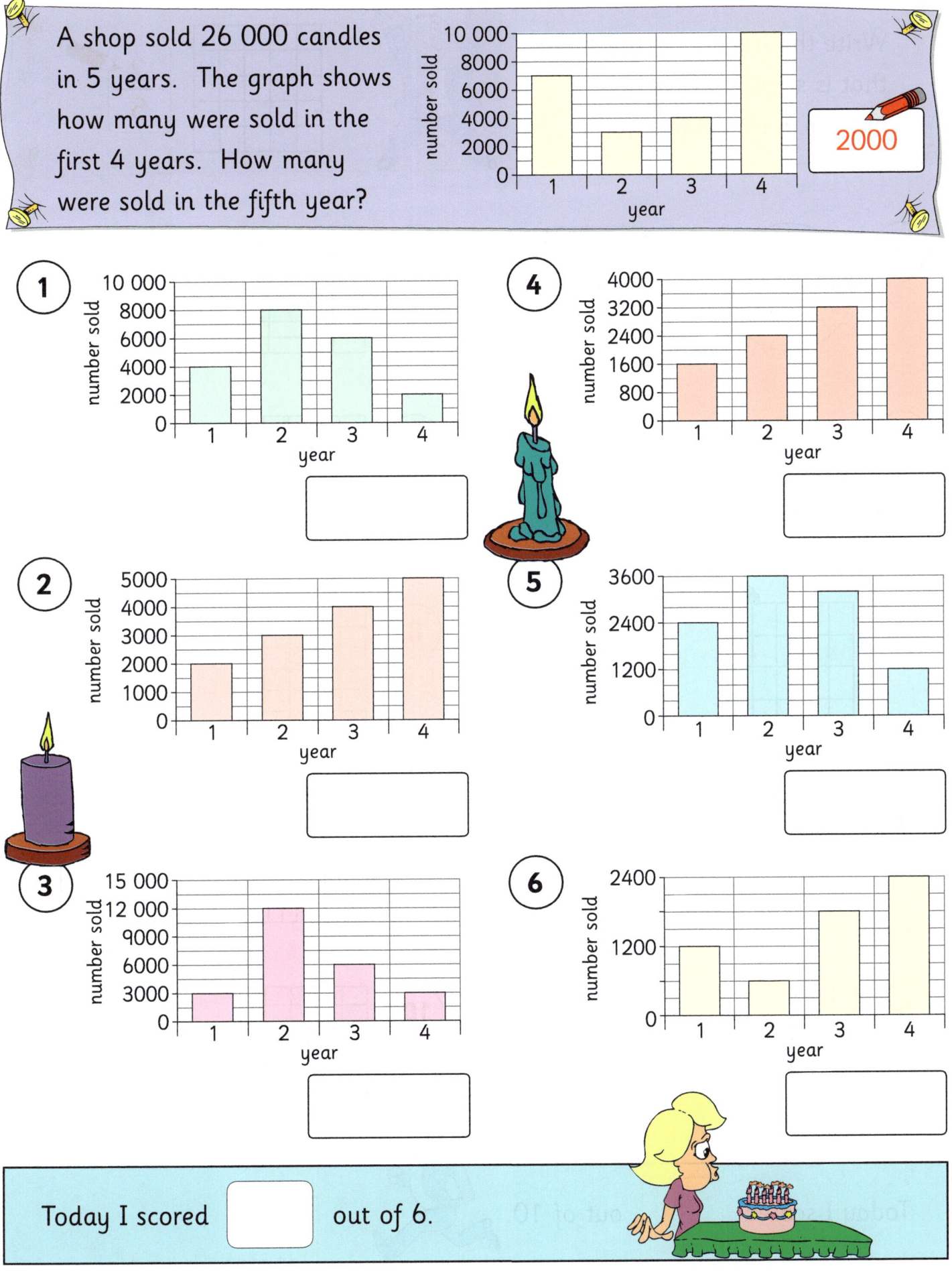

Week 12 — Day 1

Write the fraction of the shape that is shaded. Give your answer in its simplest form.

$\frac{2}{5}$

1.
2.
3.
4.
5.
6.
7.
8.
9.
10.

Today I scored ☐ out of 10.

Week 12 — Day 2

Circle the number in the box that is a prime number. 15 (29) 32

1) 4   9   13

2) 5   8   12

3) 11   14   21

4) 6   24   31

5) 40   45   59

6) 66   71   77

7) 28   47   63

8) 27   57   67

9) 33   83   93

10) 23   51   55

11) 43   75   87

12) 39   69   79

13) 9   89   99

14) 81   88   97

Today I scored ☐ out of 14.

Week 12 — Dαy 3

The table shows information about a rectangle. Complete the table.

Area	36 m²
Width	4 m
Length	9 m

1
Area	m²
Width	10 m
Length	11 m

2
Area	24 m²
Width	3 m
Length	m

3
Area	28 m²
Width	4 m
Length	m

4
Area	40 m²
Width	5 m
Length	m

5
Area	m²
Width	7 m
Length	11 m

6
Area	48 m²
Width	m
Length	8 m

7
Area	4.8 m²
Width	0.4 m
Length	m

8
Area	6.3 m²
Width	0.7 m
Length	m

9
Area	7.2 m²
Width	m
Length	12 m

10
Area	m²
Width	0.9 m
Length	12 m

Today I scored ☐ out of 10.

Week 12 — Day 4

How many sweets does each person get?

Mina divides 258 sweets between 6 people.

43 sweets

1. Tara divides 279 sweets between 9 people.

   ☐ sweets

2. Ned divides 124 sweets between 4 people.

   ☐ sweets

3. Seth divides 612 sweets between 6 people.

   ☐ sweets

4. Omar divides 255 sweets between 5 people.

   ☐ sweets

5. Keiko divides 176 sweets between 8 people.

   ☐ sweets

6. Liam divides 294 sweets between 7 people.

   ☐ sweets

7. Kenji divides 175 sweets between 7 people.

   ☐ sweets

8. Abiba divides 484 sweets between 11 people.

   ☐ sweets

9. Maru divides 477 sweets between 9 people.

   ☐ sweets

10. Femi divides 496 sweets between 8 people.

    ☐ sweets

Today I scored ☐ out of 10.

Week 12 — Day 5

Complete the calculation. 2550 + [1325] = 3875

1) 1503 + 1382 = ☐

2) ☐ − 5330 = 2319

3) 3410 + 5780 = ☐

4) 3112 + ☐ = 7895

5) ☐ − 6354 = 1622

6) ☐ + 1205 = 3614

7) ☐ − 5631 = 2814

8) 1246 + ☐ = 8791

9) ☐ − 2198 = 1010

10) 7083 − ☐ = 3652

11) 6206 + ☐ = 9075

12) ☐ − 1533 = 5761

Today I scored ☐ out of 12.

Answers

Week 1 — Day 1
1. 0.3
2. $\frac{7}{10}$ or $\frac{70}{100}$
3. 0.8
4. $\frac{1}{10}$ or $\frac{10}{100}$
5. 0.23
6. $\frac{87}{100}$
7. 0.51
8. $\frac{73}{100}$
9. 0.29
10. $\frac{13}{100}$
11. 0.02
12. $\frac{1}{100}$

Week 1 — Day 2
1. 20°
2. 55°
3. 65°
4. 102°
5. 46°
6. 74°
7. 140°
8. 35°

Week 1 — Day 3
1. 8 km
2. 15 km
3. 24 km
4. 9 km
5. 1.5 km
6. 1 km
7. 0.6 km
8. 0.3 km

Week 1 — Day 4
1. £9.00
2. £0.60
3. £3.50
4. £1.20
5. £1.80
6. £2.00
7. £0.95
8. £6.00

Week 1 — Day 5
1. 60
2. 100
3. 150
4. 36
5. 72
6. 99
7. 45
8. 147
9. 176
10. 75

Week 2 — Day 1
1. 15 000
2. 44 000
3. 75 000
4. 15 400
5. 55 000
6. 79 300
7. 82 400
8. 44 310
9. 15 090
10. 59 024
11. 10 250
12. 159 931

Week 2 — Day 2
1. 9
2. 15
3. 3
4. 8
5. 20
6. 6
7. 37
8. 14
9. 70
10. 24
11. 44
12. 39

Week 2 — Day 3
1. 2002
2. 1600
3. 1310
4. 1120
5. 1205
6. 2014
7. 1009
8. 2021
9. 1960
10. 1550
11. 1471
12. 1979

Week 2 — Day 4
1. $1\frac{1}{2}$ hours
2. $1\frac{1}{2}$ hours
3. 2 hours
4. $4\frac{1}{2}$ hours
5. $8\frac{3}{4}$ hours
6. $1\frac{1}{3}$ hours
7. 8 hours
8. $2\frac{2}{3}$ hours

Week 2 — Day 5
1. 24 cm
2. 10 cm
3. 16 cm
4. 9 cm
5. 80 cm
6. 40 cm
7. 280 cm
8. 2 cm

Week 3 — Day 1
1. 2, 2
2. 2, 2
3. 8, 8
4. 0, 0
5. 2, 4
6. 4, 2
7. 2, 0
8. 1, 1

Week 3 — Day 2
1. April and May, 8308
2. May and June, 2973
3. March and June, 7824
4. April and May, 2949
5. March and April, 1288
6. March and May, 6560
7. March and June, 7425
8. April and May, 5077
9. April and June, 10 887

Week 3 — Day 3
1. 2
2. 5
3. 2
4. 3
5. 3
6. 17
7. 2, 2
8. 2, 3 or 3, 2
9. 3, 3
10. 3, 3
11. 2, 3 or 3, 2
12. 3, 13 or 13, 3

Week 3 — Day 4
1. 75 ft
2. 45 ft
3. 22.5 ft
4. 400 m
5. 60 m
6. 120 m
7. 40 km
8. 150 miles
9. 320 km
10. 400 miles
11. 2400 km
12. 6000 miles

Week 3 — Day 5

1.
Prime number	13
Prime factor of 15	5
Composite number	6

2.
Prime number	2
Prime factor of 49	7
Composite number	10

3.
Prime number	3
Prime factor of 22	11
Composite number	4

4.
Prime number	17
Prime factor of 45	3
Composite number	15

5.
Prime number	5
Prime factor of 81	3
Composite number	9

6.
Prime number	19
Prime factor of 60	5
Composite number	12

7.
Prime number	11
Prime factor of 96	3
Composite number	14

8.
Prime number	23
Prime factor of 38	19
Composite number	21

Week 4 — Day 1
1. Neither
2. Square number
3. Cube number
4. Neither
5. Square number
6. Square number
7. Cube number
8. Neither
9. Square number
10. Square number

Week 4 — Day 2
1. 14:15
2. 09:05
3. 13:30
4. 15:15
5. 13:05
6. 16:10
7. 19:25
8. 20:15
9. 21:06
10. 17:21

Week 4 — Day 3
1. 78, 73, 68, 63
2. 146, 157, 168, 179
3. 360, 465, 570, 675
4. 464, 324, 184, 44
5. 234, 213, 192, 171
6. 440, 465, 490, 515
7. 463, 351, 239, 127
8. 674, 751, 828, 905

Week 4 — Day 4
1. $3^2 = 3 \times 3 = $ **9**
2. $2^3 = 2 \times 2 \times 2 = $ **8**
3. $5^2 = 5 \times 5 = $ **25**
4. $4^2 = $ **4 × 4** $ = 16$
5. $9^2 = $ **9 × 9** $ = $ **81**
6. $4^3 = 4 \times 4 \times 4 = $ **64**
7. $1^2 = $ **1 × 1** $ = 1$
8. $11^2 = 121$
9. $6^3 = 6 \times 6 \times $ **6** $ = 216$
10. $10^3 = $ **1000**

Week 4 — Day 5
1. 115°
2. 61°
3. 26°
4. 58°
5. 154°
6. 50°
7. 8°
8. 80°
9. 17°
10. 188°

Week 5 — Day 1
1. 6 × 5
2. 4^2
3. 8 × 5
4. 7^2
5. 10^2
6. 7 × 10
7. 8 × 11
8. 3^2
9. $3^2 \times 4$
10. 7×2^2
11. 4^3
12. 11 × 12

Week 5 — Day 2
1. $\frac{2}{12}$
2. $\frac{2}{5}$
3. $\frac{10}{25}$
4. $\frac{16}{24}$
5. $\frac{6}{24}$
6. $\frac{16}{28}$
7. $\frac{16}{20}$
8. $\frac{44}{77}$
9. $\frac{25}{35}$
10. $\frac{2}{5}$
11. $\frac{3}{60}$
12. $\frac{100}{150}$

Week 5 — Day 3
1. 10 000
2. 40 000
3. 15 000
4. 35 000
5. 16 000
6. 85 000
7. 49 000
8. 24 000

Week 5 — Day 4
1. Factors: 3, 6
   Multiples: 36, 60
2. Factors: 3
   Multiples: 27, 72
3. Factors: 2, 5
   Multiples: 30, 100
4. Factors: 4, 2
   Multiples: 72, 56
5. Factors: none
   Multiples: 88, 55, 121
6. Factors: 2, 7
   Multiples: 140, 70
7. Factors: 3, 5
   Multiples: 45, 60
8. Factors: 4, 10, 5
   Multiples: 80
9. Factors: 5
   Multiples: 100, 75
10. Factors: 20, 5, 12, 3
    Multiples: 120
11. Factors: 6, 12, 3
    Multiples: 48
12. Factors: 25, 5
    Multiples: 400

Week 5 — Day 5
1. 7 days, 2 hours, 35 minutes
2. 15 days, 14 hours, 5 minutes
3. 25 days, 8 hours, 0 minutes
4. 30 days, 0 hours, 50 minutes
5. 38 days, 16 hours, 22 minutes
6. 31 days, 0 hours, 7 minutes
7. 16 days, 2 hours, 20 minutes
8. 7 days, 8 hours, 9 minutes

Week 6 — Day 1
1. 8000
2. 52
3. 350 000
4. 8.7
5. 3200
6. 45
7. 490
8. 7200
9. 2326
10. 24 710
11. 72 000
12. 793 400
13. 14 400
14. 60 000

Week 6 — Day 2
1. 20 °C, 15 °C
2. 16 °C, 8 °C
3. −1 °C, 7 °C
4. −3 °C, 18 °C

Week 6 — Day 3
1. 2.1 km
2. 2.5 km
3. 4.5 km
4. 8.4 km
5. 8.3 km
6. 11.4 km
7. 8.15 km
8. 7.25 km
9. 6.92 km
10. 4.85 km

Week 6 — Day 4
1. 20 cm²
2. 130 cm²
3. 55 cm²
4. 200 cm²
5. 70 cm²
6. 45 cm²
7. 72 cm²
8. 72 cm²

Week 6 — Day 5
1. 2
2. 10
3. 6
4. 3
5. 6
6. 12
7. 33

63

Week 7 — Day 1

1.
2.
3.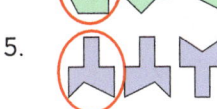
4.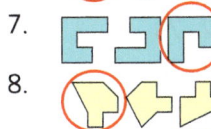
5.
6.
7.
8.
9.
10.

Week 7 — Day 2

1. 0.03 and $\frac{3}{100}$
2. 0.16 and $\frac{16}{100}$
3. 0.7 and $\frac{7}{10}$
4. 0.455 and $\frac{455}{1000}$
5. 0.205 and $\frac{205}{1000}$
6. 0.05 and $\frac{5}{100}$
7. 0.101 and $\frac{101}{1000}$
8. 0.52 and $\frac{520}{1000}$
9. 0.65 and $\frac{65}{100}$
10. 0.214 and $\frac{214}{1000}$
11. 0.008 and $\frac{8}{1000}$
12. 1.001 and $\frac{1001}{1000}$

Week 7 — Day 3

1. A to B: 2 left
   A to C: 4 up
2. A to B: 3 right and 1 up
   A to C: 2 right and 4 up
3. A to B: 6 down
   A to C: 3 left and 4 down
4. A to B: 3 left and 5 down
   A to C: 1 right and 4 down
5. A to B: 4 right and 1 down
   A to C: 2 right and 5 down
6. A to B: 2 left and 2 up
   A to C: 4 left and 3 down

Week 7 — Day 4

1. 1.614
2. 1.211
3. 1.595
4. 2.341
5. 5.5
6. 3.078
7. 5.64
8. 4.014
9. 6.005
10. 1.002
11. 12.98
12. 10.4

Week 7 — Day 5

1. A: (4, 1)
   B: (7, 3)
2. A: (6, 7)
   B: (7, 5)
3. A: (2, 7)
   B: (7, 6)
4. A: (3, 7)
   B: (0, 4)
5. A: (6, 0)
   B: (6, 1)
6. A: (0, 6)
   B: (2, 0)

Week 8 — Day 1

1. rectangle, 6 faces
2. circle, 3 faces
3. circle, 2 faces
4. square, 5 faces
5. square (or rectangle), 5 faces
6. triangle, 4 faces
7. hexagon, 8 faces
8. pentagon, 7 faces

Week 8 — Day 2

1. 0.8 l, 800 ml
2. 1.4 l, 1400 ml
3. 0.3 l, 300 ml
4. 0.75 l, 750 ml
5. 1.5 l, 1500 ml
6. 0.35 l, 350 ml
7. 0.2 l, 200 ml
8. 0.125 l, 125 ml

Week 8 — Day 3

1. 1.843, 1.833, 2.238
2. 5.654
3. 8.822, 8.283
4. 9.482
5. 7.021, 7.022, 7.21
6. 2.705, 2.75, 2.57
7. 0.006, 0.05, 0.6
8. 6.95, 6.592
9. 2.367, 2.463
10. 4.22, 4.202
11. 9.879, 9.799, 9.798
12. 6.51

Week 8 — Day 4

1. 7.55 m
2. 545.7 cm
3. 2.504 m
4. 3.113 m
5. 4.974 m
6. 8.905 m

Week 8 — Day 5

1. 0.2 l
2. 0.25 l
3. 0.5 l
4. 0.2 l
5. 0.3 l
6. 0.2 l
7. 0.1 l
8. 0.5 l
9. 0.1 l

Week 9 — Day 1

1. 25%
2. 60%
3. 10%
4. 5%
5. 20%
6. 100%
7. 40%
8. 80%
9. 80%
10. 50%
11. 80%
12. 4%

Week 9 — Day 2

1. 160°
2. 80°
3. 45°
4. 340°
5. 95°
6. 20°
7. 255°
8. 115°
9. 25°
10. 195°

Week 9 — Day 3

1. 43%
2. 20%
3. 30%
4. 12%
5. 15%
6. 21%
7. 32%
8. 48%
9. 94%
10. 87%

Week 9 — Day 4

1. 2
2. 3
3. 8
4. 15
5. 8
6. 18
7. 8
8. 9

Week 9 — Day 5

1. 40%, 0.45, $\frac{50}{100}$
2. 5%, 0.5, $\frac{55}{100}$
3. $\frac{6}{10}$, 0.63, 66%
4. 0.2, $\frac{1}{4}$, 27%
5. 70%, $\frac{15}{20}$, 0.8
6. 0.3, $\frac{2}{5}$, 45%
7. $\frac{40}{50}$, 0.85, 90%
8. 36%, 0.39, $\frac{10}{25}$

Week 10 — Day 1
1. 4 cm, 40°
2. 2 cm, 20°
3. 6 cm, 45°
4. 8.5 cm, 142°
5. 18.5 cm, 65°
6. 2.22 m, 123°
7. 3.04 m, 71°
8. 1.7 m, 270°

Week 10 — Day 2
1. 3, 3.5
2. 7, 6.6
3. 13, 12.9
4. 22, 21.5
5. 79, 78.7
6. 102, 102.1
7. 231, 231.0
8. 674, 674.0

Week 10 — Day 3
1. 3 in
2. 250 cm
3. 150 cm
4. 45 cm
5. 5 ft 0 in
6. 4 ft 2 in
7. 275 cm
8. 11 ft 8 in
9. 0.5 cm
10. 100 ft 0 in

Week 10 — Day 4
1. $\frac{2}{3}$
2. $\frac{2}{5}$
3. $\frac{5}{8}$
4. $\frac{7}{10}$
5. $1\frac{1}{6}$
6. $\frac{1}{12}$
7. $1\frac{6}{15}$ (or $1\frac{2}{5}$)
8. $\frac{7}{18}$
9. $1\frac{13}{24}$
10. $\frac{7}{30}$
11. $1\frac{3}{60}$ (or $1\frac{1}{20}$)
12. $\frac{51}{100}$
13. $1\frac{19}{56}$
14. $\frac{91}{108}$

Week 10 — Day 5
1. 10
2. 5
3. 18%
4. 48%
5. 2
6. 3
7. 15%
8. 6
9. 19%
10. 90%

Week 11 — Day 1
1. 24
2. 7
3. 77
4. 60
5. 100
6. 30
7. 1600
8. 9
9. 2500
10. 80
11. 500
12. 70

Week 11 — Day 2
1. 317°
2. 195°
3. 338°
4. 270°
5. 215°
6. 199°
7. 319°
8. 246°
9. 172°

Week 11 — Day 3
1. 70 minutes
2. 24 minutes
3. 140 minutes
4. 60 hours
5. 42 hours
6. 248 hours
7. 36 minutes
8. 400 minutes
9. 230 minutes
10. 86 hours

Week 11 — Day 4
1. 32 ÷ 2
2. 64 ÷ 8
3. 4 × 9
4. 9 × 3
5. 13 × 2
6. 4 × 16
7. 11^2
8. 29 × 2
9. 500 × 2

Week 11 — Day 5
1. 6000
2. 12 000
3. 2000
4. 14 800
5. 15 600
6. 20 000

Week 12 — Day 1
1. $\frac{3}{4}$
2. $\frac{1}{2}$
3. $\frac{1}{4}$
4. $\frac{1}{3}$
5. $\frac{2}{3}$
6. $\frac{3}{8}$
7. $\frac{2}{5}$
8. $\frac{3}{10}$
9. $\frac{2}{9}$
10. $\frac{2}{7}$

Week 12 — Day 2
1. 13
2. 5
3. 11
4. 31
5. 59
6. 71
7. 47
8. 67
9. 83
10. 23
11. 43
12. 79
13. 89
14. 97

Week 12 — Day 3
1. 110 m²
2. 8 m
3. 7 m
4. 8 m
5. 77 m²
6. 6 m
7. 12 m
8. 9 m
9. 0.6 m
10. 10.8 m²

Week 12 — Day 4
1. 31 sweets
2. 31 sweets
3. 102 sweets
4. 51 sweets
5. 22 sweets
6. 42 sweets
7. 25 sweets
8. 44 sweets
9. 53 sweets
10. 62 sweets

Week 12 — Day 5
1. 2885
2. 7649
3. 9190
4. 4783
5. 7976
6. 2409
7. 8445
8. 7545
9. 3208
10. 3431
11. 2869
12. 7294